10 0???10 7

UNIVERSI

WIT

D1587976

A NATIONAL THEATRE

Books *by* Harley Granville-Barker

Plays
*The Marrying of Ann Leete.
*The Voysey Inheritance. (Revised 1913.)
*Waste. (Rewritten 1926.)
*The Madras House. (Revised 1925.)
*Rococo: Vote by Ballot: Farewell to the Theatre.
  (Three one-act plays.) 1917.
*The Secret Life. 1923.
*His Majesty. 1928.

With LAURENCE HOUSMAN
*Prunella: or, Love in a Dutch Garden. 1906.

With DION CLAYTON CALTHROP
*The Harlequinade. 1918.

English Versions of Foreign Plays
*Anatol: *by* Arthur Schnitzler. 1911.
Deburau: *by* Sacha Guitry. 1921.
Doctor Knock: *by* Jules Romains. 1925.
*Six Gentlemen in a Row: *by* Jules Romains. 1927.

With HELEN GRANVILLE-BARKER
*The Kingdom of God. 1927.
*The Romantic Young Lady: *by* Gregorio Martinez
  Sierra. 1929.
*The Women have their Way: A Hundred Years Old:
  Fortunato: The Lady from Alfaqueque: *by*
  Serafín and Joaquín Alvarez Quintero. 1927.

Criticism
*The Exemplary Theatre. 1922.
From Henry V to Hamlet.
*Prefaces to Shakespeare: First Series. 1927.
*Prefaces to Shakespeare: Second Series. 1930.

---

*Published by Sidgwick & Jackson, Ltd.

A National Theatre

by

Harley Granville-Barker

London
Sidgwick & Jackson, Ltd.
1930

Printed in Great Britain at
The Westminster Press
411a Harrow Road
London W.9

CONTENTS

⁎ *The Plans will be found at the end of the book.*

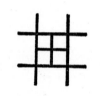

PREFACE

S O M E twenty-seven years ago William Archer and I—the bulk of the work being his—drew up *A Scheme and Estimates for a National Theatre.* It was printed and circulated privately with this endorsement on its flyleaf:

> Having read and carefully considered this scheme for a National Theatre, we desire to express our belief that such an institution is urgently needed, and that it could in all probability be successfully established on the general lines here indicated.
>
> HENRY IRVING
> SQUIRE BANCROFT
> J. M. BARRIE
> HELEN D'OYLY CARTE
> JOHN HARE
> HENRY ARTHUR JONES
> A. W. PINERO

The notion was that, thus encouraged, some benevolent millionaire might find the £350,000 or so wanted (and I seem to remember Archer making a journey to Skibo to talk to Mr. Andrew Carnegie about it), and would prefer his handsome gift to the nation to be unheralded. Nothing came of this. Then the book, which could hardly command readers for its own sake, was public-spiritedly published by Messrs. Duckworth, on the chance that some unreckoned-with millionaire might hear of it and, as the bankers say, " do the needful." Nothing came of that either; though I believe the scheme

vii

did in some sort serve as a text-book for the dis-
cussions of the National Theatre (Shakespeare
Memorial) Committee, then newly formed, and
another would-be operator in the millionaire-
market. But in a few years' time the estimates were
out of date; even before the war prices had risen,
the Cinema and American competition bringing
many changes. We talked of revising them, for we
never doubted but that the theatre's time would
come. Instead came the war and its consequences,
and the old figures ceased to bear any relation
whatever to facts. In the years following Archer
was keen for something to be done, anything that
would help give back to the theatre he had served
so well some of the self-respect he sadly felt it to
have lost. And he did what he could, more (this
was like him) because he felt it his duty to than
with any immediate hope of success. Then he died.
It has been left to me—prospects now showing a
little brighter—to re-state our case.

I am as confident as he was, and as I always have
been, that, if not to-day or to-morrow, some day or
other something that answers to a National Theatre
will be set up in England. There is apparently no
other way by which the best of our drama can be
kept in being. And no one, noting the large part
now played in education by drama and dramatic
method—to distinguish no other tendency—can
doubt, surely, that a generation will rise, if it has
not already risen, to whom such a theatre will seem
a necessity.* One need not be impatient. The fear
is rather, since its establishing with its complex

* And a further development of this may be studied in the
striking report on the Drama made by the Adult Education
Committee of the Board of Education and published in 1926.

machinery is admittedly a difficult, and in England an unprecedented, task, that timid and divided counsels may lead to the starting of some inept and addled enterprise, whose failure, and the cost of it, will discredit the idea for years to come.

The demand for a National Theatre long antedates the preparation of the *Scheme and Estimates*. Matthew Arnold, his imagination stirred by the visit of the Comédie Française, was urging it in 1880.

" We have in England (he writes) everything to make us dissatisfied with the chaotic and ineffective condition into which our stage has fallen. We have the remembrance of better things in the past, and the elements for better things in the future. We have a splendid national drama of the Elizabethan age, and a later drama which has no lack of pieces conspicuous by their stage qualities, their vivacity and their talent, and interesting by their pictures of manners.* We have had great actors. We have good actors not a few at the present moment. But we have been unlucky, as we so often are, in the work of organisation. . . . It seems to me that every one of us is concerned to find a remedy for this melancholy state of things, and that the pleasure we have had in the visit of the French company is barren unless it leaves us with the impulse to do so, and with the lesson how alone it can be rationally done. ' Forget '—can we not hear those fine artists saying in an undertone to us amidst their graceful compliments of adieu?— ' forget your clap-trap, and believe that the State, the nation in its collective and corporate character, does well to concern itself about an influence so important to national life and manners as the theatre. . . . The people *will* have the theatre; then make it a good one. . . . The theatre is irresistible; organise the theatre.' "

* And if this could be said in 1880 we have how much more to boast of now!

This also found place upon a flyleaf of our book in 1907, and I quote it again; for in 1930 it is as trenchantly true as ever, and yet more pertinent now that there is a better theatre to organise than the one which Matthew Arnold knew. The demand was recurrent through the eighteen-eighties and -nineties and through the first years of the new century; and these were the years when English drama, under private enterprise, was making great strides. Yet the very dramatists and managers who were most successful under those conditions—Pinero, Henry Arthur Jones, and, later, Bernard Shaw; Irving, Hare, and Beerbohm Tree—were foremost in asserting the need for something more. A concrete and detailed plan was lacking; and, without pretending that it was the only possible plan, the *Scheme and Estimates*, drawn up to fit the circumstances of that time, supplied one. These have radically changed. Without claiming perfection for it, here is another adjusted to the circumstances of this.

Much of the old scheme has been retained; the provision for the government and management of the theatre, for the pension fund, the triumvirate for the choice of plays, the fee system for the actors. But (apart from the fact that a quarter of a century's experience and observation should have taught one something!) the drastic change in the cost of every sort of material and service that the theatre would need, coupled with the impossibility of appreciably raising the prices at which the product can be sold, make it necessary to re-construct the whole affair on a wider basis. As one of my critics puts it, assentingly so far: The day of the small workshop is over—in this as in other business. Anyone disposed to think the plan as it now stands too big, should work out his reduction of it, price-list in hand, so to speak. There is, I can assure him, no megalomania involved. The scale of the organisation, with its every detail, has been dictated simply by the economic necessities of the case. If you want a theatre of this sort you must have a theatre of this size and capitalise it to this extent. That is, I believe, the lesson which even a casual glance at things theatrical in England and America and at the condition of similar theatres on the Continent to-day will teach. But it should be in no way a deterrent lesson. It implies a better theatre as well as a bigger, none the less wanted and only the more fitted to satisfy the want.

I have, needless to say, run up a long list of debts for help and information; my own, in matters theatrical, not being very immediate now-adays—but, possibly, I see the situation in a juster perspective because of that. I owe thanks for information about theatres abroad to the Austrian Minister in London, to Dr. Alexandre Hevesi, director of the National Theatre in Budapest, to M. Jacques Copeau, to Mr. J. R. Cahill, Commercial Counsellor at our Embassy in Paris, to Mr. R. J. Bowker of our Embassy in Berlin. For information about the 'Old Vic' I have to thank Lord Lytton, the chairman of its governing body; and Sir Barry Jackson and Mr. C. B. Cochran gave me similar help. Mr. R. Golding Bright, whose knowledge of things theatrical, particularly from the dramatist's point of view, covers many years, has been good enough to read the proofs and definitely to approve the scheme so far as the dramatists' interests are concerned. While I was at work a committee, under Lord Lytton's chairmanship, was also engaged in drawing up a

National Theatre scheme for submission to the Prime Minister. I was allowed some news of their proceedings, and I do not think their conclusions differ widely from mine. I am in debt to Mr. Geoffrey Whitworth for much and varied assistance, and for even more to Mr. Walter Peacock, who went to great trouble in giving and getting and testing for me every sort of detail of the running expenses of London theatres to-day. I cannot be sufficiently grateful to him. Mr. W. L. Somerville of Toronto has kindly allowed me to reproduce his prize designs for a National Theatre, and Mr. P. Morley-Horder was good enough to make a rough estimate of the cost of carrying them out upon some site in London. I have to thank Mr. David Turpie for checking all my calculations.

Lastly, I owe particular thanks to Sir Alfred Butt, Mr. Horace Watson, Mr. Alec L. Rea and his partner Mr. E. P. Clift, and Mr. H. M. Harwood, who were good enough to consider the scheme as it was first elaborated and to criticise it in detail. A summary of their opinions will be found in Appendix I. No one having any knowledge of theatrical London will need to be told with what authority they speak; Sir Alfred Butt as a controller of enterprises upon the largest scale; Mr. Horace Watson, responsibly connected for forty years with the Haymarket Theatre, whose mere amenities are probably unrivalled in Europe; Mr. Alec Rea and Mr. Clift, whose recent experience ranges from their permanent management of the St. Martin's Theatre to a variety of larger productions elsewhere; and Mr. H. M. Harwood, possibly a unique combination of playwright, theatre-manager and man of business. H. G.-B.

Paris, February 1930.

Last October the British Drama League sent a
circular letter to a select number of people asking
them whether, without committing themselves to
any particular method of finance or organisation,
they were in favour of a National Theatre. The list
of those who said they were is, I think, worth setting down again.

Mr. Lascelles Abercrombie Viscount Allenby
Mr. Henry Ainley Mr. Norman Angell
Mr. Charles Aitken Miss Lena Ashwell
The Revd. Cyril Alington Mr. Robert Atkins
Sir Hugh Allen

Mr. Stanley Baldwin Dr. F. S. Boas
Professor Ernest Barker Mr. Gordon Bottomley
Mr. Kenneth Barnes Dr. Cloudesley Brereton
Sir James Barrie The Hon. Oliver Brett
Mr. E. A. Baughan Sir Harry Brittain
Mr. Clifford Bax Mr. Ivor Brown
Miss Lilian Baylis Mr. Maurice Browne
Mr. Robert Anning Bell Mr. John Buchan
The Revd. Sidney M. Berry Viscount Burnham
Mr. G. W. Bishop The Right Rev. Bishop Bury

M. Emile Cammaerts Mr. Winston S. Churchill
Professor E. T. Campagnac Mr. C. B. Cochran
Professor A. Y. Campbell Mr. Sydney C. Cockerell
Mr. Lewis Casson Mr. Philip Connard
Mr. G. K. Chesterton Mr. Duff Cooper
The Bishop of Chichester Mrs. W. L. Courtney
Dr. Bernard Childs The Marquis of Crewe

Mr. W. H. Darlington Professor E. J. Dent
Archbishop Lord Davidson Mr. F. E. Doran
Mr. Basil Dean Mr. John Drinkwater
The Revd. Percy Dearmer Mr. Ashley Dukes
Lady Denman Lord Dunsany

Sir Edward Elgar

Mr. James B. Fagan
Mr. H. A. L. Fisher
Mr. Archibald Flower

Mr. John Galsworthy
Mr. Edward Garnett
Mr. J. L. Garvin
Lord Gorell
Captain Harry Graham

Sir Robert Hadfield
Sir Henry Hadow
Mr. J. L. Hammond
Captain Martin Hardie
Lt.-Col. Cuthbert Headlam
Sir George Henschel

Professor L. P. Jacks

Dame Madge Kendal
Lieut.-Com. Kenworthy
Dr. C. W. Kimmins

Mr. Harold Laski
Mr. Shane Leslie
Sir Oliver Lodge
Mr. Robert Loraine

Mr. Desmond MacCarthy
Dr. J. W. Mackail
Mr. Reginald McKenna
Mr. Compton Mackenzie
Sir Donald Maclean
Miss Margaret Macmillan

Mr. St. John Ervine

Miss Elsie Fogerty
Sir Johnston Forbes-
    Robertson

Sir Philip Ben Greet
Lady Gregory
Mr. James R. Gregson
Mr. J. T. Grein
Dr. L. Haden Guest

Mr. Carl Hentschel
Mr. J. W. Hills
Professor J. A. Hobson
Miss A. E. Horniman
Mr. Laurence Housman
Mr. Aldous Huxley

Sir Barry Jackson

Miss Gertrude Kingston
Mr. Holford Knight

Sir Sidney Low
Dame Beatrix Lyall
The Earl of Lytton

Mr. Cyril Maude
Sir Frank Meyer
Mr. Nugent Monck
Mr. A. N. Monkhouse
The Duke of Montrose
Principal A. E. Morgan

Mr. Miles Malleson
Mr. J. J. Mallon
Colonel Malone
Mr. Edward Marsh
Mr. W. Lee Mathews

Sir Robert Newman
Mr. Robert Nichols

Mr. Conal O'Riordan
The Hon. W. G. Ormsby-
  Gore

Sir Bernard Partridge
Lord Eustace Percy
Mr. Eden Phillpotts
The Rev. Arnold Pinchard

Mr. Roger Quilter

Captain Herbert Read
Sir Harry Reichel
Professor C. H. Reilly
Dr. Ernest Rhys
Mr. Charles Ricketts
Professor J. G. Robertson
Miss Elizabeth Robins

Sir Michael Sadler
Professor Ernest de Selin-
  court
Mr. George Sheringham

Dame Meriel Talbot
Mr. R. H. Tawney
Miss Marie Tempest
Mr. Charles Tennyson

The Hon. Evan Morgan
Mr. Charles Morgan
Mr. P. Morley-Horder
Mr. J. Ramsay Muir
Professor Gilbert Murray

Professor Allardyce Nicoll
Mr. Cyril Norwood

The Countess of Oxford

Sir Arthur Pinero
Sir Nigel Playfair
Professor A. W. Pollard
Sir Frederick Pollock

Mr. Lennox Robinson
Professor William Rothen-
  stein
Captain R. P. P. Rowe
Mr. B. Seebohm Rowntree
Mr. Albert Rutherston

Mrs. Philip Snowden
Mr. J. C. Squire
Mr. Frank Swinnerton

Dr. C. Sanford Terry
Miss Sybil Thorndike
Mr. Arnold Toynbee
Mr. W. J. Turner

xv

Major Frank Vernon

Sir Lawrence Weaver   Sir Robert Witt
Mr. Norman Wilkinson   Mr. P. G. Wodehouse
Dr. R. Vaughan Williams   Dr. C. Hagberg Wright
Professor J. Dover Wilson

Sir Arthur Yapp   Sir Francis Younghusband
The Archbishop of York

It is a mixed bag, truly; but the better for that. About every calling and school of thought in England must be represented. As the canvass was a preliminary to approaching the present Labour Government, none of its members were asked for an opinion, but several of them have since gone out of the way to give a favourable one. I do not think such a variety of influential support would have been forthcoming till now. It really looks as if the National Theatre were on its way.

CHAPTER I

THE NEED FOR A NATIONAL THEATRE

W H A T need is there for a National Theatre?
What need is there of the National Gallery, or the
British Museum, or for chairs of English Literature
in the Universities? We could get on somehow
without them, and a number of people would never
even know they had been abolished. What need is
there for St. Paul's Cathedral? The land could be
profitably sold and a few hundred cheap brick
churches built and endowed out of the proceeds.
The answer—churchman and sceptic alike would
give it—is that St. Paul's stands as a symbol, and
not of the Christian faith only, but of the dignity
of spiritual power. The advocate for a National
Theatre can plead its mere utility, can show that
it will do what no other theatre is likely to. But he
had better take yet higher ground. He must plead
for the drama as something more than casual entertainment, as an art worthy to rank with other fine
arts, and as having its spiritual functions too.
Neither art nor literature, nor even religion, are
always on the heights, nor need they be. But they
need to have the heights in view. The drama, with
its fellow arts, is an easy prey to the conscience-
less tradesman, and the honest tradesman cannot
unaided bring it salvation. It suffers in repute,
even as do literature and religion, from the cheap-
jack and the charlatan. A National Theatre would
be its cathedral, and stand, as nothing else could,
for a witness to the honour in which, well deserving,

I   B

it should be held, and for a perpetual encouragement.

English drama ranks high among the literatures
of the world. English acting, given its chance, can
compare with the best; but the English nation, as a
nation, apparently cares nothing for the credit of
either. The foreigner, the American, and the visitor
from the Dominions will probably find the Theatre
Royal, Drury Lane, our National Theatre of the
past, occupied (quite legitimately as things are) by
American musical comedy; they must seek for
Shakespeare in the slums; and, for anything that
can be called representative modern drama, they
may, as often as not, seek everywhere in vain. This
is something of a reproach, surely, to a civilised
community and the capital city of an Empire.

The need for a National Theatre is patent enough
—if, that is to say, there is any real need for good
drama well done. Some people honestly do not
think it matters very much whether you have good
drama or bad, or, when you have good drama,
whether you have it well done or ill. Most of them,
however, have not really thought about the matter
at all; the majority of us do not think imagina-
tively, except at a crisis, about our own affairs.
One brings them into the argument because it
by no means follows that when good drama well
done is there to hand they will not quickly come to
like it, even to wondering how they ever did without it. If the Comédie Française, the Schauspielhaus in Vienna, the Royal Theatre at Copenhagen,
and the rest had never existed, we should not find
crowds rioting in the streets and refusing to pay
any taxes but the one tax that would endow them.
Yet there would be a pretty row if the French or
the Danish or even the Austrian Government in its

poverty set out to abolish them now. British Museums and National Galleries and National Theatres are established because an imaginative minority resolves that they ought to be.

The minority in favour of a National Theatre has grown greatly during the last twenty-five years, in numbers, influence, and—more importantly—in appreciation of what it is that is wanted, and why. Objection in principle to the endowment of drama has probably all but vanished; so, at least, we may suppose when we find such a stalwart individualist as Mr. Reginald McKenna one of the sponsors of the rebuilding and endowing of the Shakespeare Memorial Theatre at Stratford. Though they committed themselves to no precise method of endowment, the long list of names recently secured by the British Drama League in support of the project is sufficiently imposing: Archbishop Lord Davidson, the Archbishop of York, and the Bishop of Chichester, Mr. Baldwin and Mr. Winston Churchill, Lord Crewe, Mr. McKenna and Sir Donald Maclean, Lord Allenby, Sir Frederick Pollock, Mr. Garvin, Sir Robert Hadfield, the Headmasters of Eton and Harrow, Lord Eustace Percy and Mr. Fisher (and Sir Charles Trevelyan could be added; a solid twelve years in its favour at the Board of Education), Sir Edward Elgar, Sir James Barrie and Mr. Galsworthy, Sir Arthur Pinero, Sir Johnston Forbes-Robertson, M.P.s of all parties—only a tithe of the names have been quoted; and though the present Government was deliberately left uncanvassed, Mr. Clynes, the Home Secretary, bore lengthy testimony to his belief in it. Then among the rank and file of supporters (these must be in mere numbers—even in voting strength!—far from negligible) are the inspirers and guiders of the re-

3

markable post-war movement of amateurs of drama, who in every town and village, every college and school, every factory in England (it would almost seem) now read, discuss, and act plays among themselves, with a taste that ranges from Aeschylus to —whatever modern dramatist may be said to be least like him, with a range from competence to incompetence that is almost as wide, but with an enthusiasm that is very genuine. The positive artistic product of this nation-wide field of amateur drama may not, often, be of a very high quality; in the nature of things it cannot be. But there could be no more fruitful education in taste, no better breeding of the audiences to which a National Theatre will appeal.

Private Enterprise and its Handicaps

Not that there is ever any lack of a public for good drama well done, or likely to be. " Then how is it," asks the innocent objector, " that private enterprise cannot supply all you want and make a legitimate profit by doing so? " One could counter very simply with the argument from experience. Private enterprise never has been able to do this with any completeness; and it has not been for lack of trying. The commercial manager, so-called, is not invariably—strange though this may appear! —a man whose single idea it is to make as much money as possible by the shabbiest means. He may have an excellent taste in plays; after all, he has produced some fairly good ones in his time. But his business is to make money. And the more individual the enterprise the more it is a risky one. And the capital is seldom all his own.

It would take too long to follow out the intricacies of London theatrical finance; but a few rays of light may suffice. The owning, even the leasing of a theatre and the producing of plays in it are nowadays seldom an identical enterprise. There is little that is risky in *owning* a popular theatre; though truly, as it is known to be profitable property, it is made the prey of every public authority with a rate to raise or a tax to levy (the London Water Board, when it was first constituted, openly confessed to making the West-End theatres fill up a deficit in its budget on the ground that ' they could afford to pay '). So profitable is this side of the business that to many of the theatres there are two, three, four, even five profit rentals, more or less concealed, all of which the enterprise of play producing must carry. The successful play can carry them, and everyone is happy. The failures must carry them too; whatever else happens rent must be paid—and in advance.

It is the producer of the play who does the speculating. He may be on shares with the manager of the theatre, but the contract will provide for his speedy exit into the street with bag and baggage if the takings are not enough to cover the rent—out of which, as aforesaid, three or four people may be taking toll before it reaches the real landlord—and other front-of-the-house outgoings, calculable almost to a sovereign before the contract is made. The producer can be sure of nothing. He makes rough estimates of the cost of his scenery and dresses, his cast, his rehearsals. If he knows his job he should not be more than twenty-five per cent out; but that asks nice reckoning, for with every play these things vary, and there will be all sorts of emergencies. Success may be definite and immediate; but this must mean audiences numbering six thousand or so a week; more, if the theatre is a large

one and the production really costly. An unequivo-
cal success is expected to attract anything from one
hundred thousand to five hundred thousand people.
Suppose a publisher had to sell that number of
copies of a book before he could call it successful.
Even so, he would have the British Isles for his
field and an unlimited time in which to sell them.
But a theatre must gather in Londoners at the rate
of from five to fifteen hundred and more a night.
If a hundred thousand people want to see a play,
and they distribute their attendance over six
months, it is a failure. If only fifty thousand people
want to see it and, having other occupations, need
three or four months' latitude, long before this the
enterprising producer will find himself in the street,
glad to sell a £2,000 production for a £20 note,
sooner than let it rot away at yet more cost to him
in some store. The theatre with its four landlords
will have found another tenant; its manager will be
philosophical, for even though you are paying your
rent four times over (so to speak) you have your
theatre, and that is something. The producer will
have his £20 note to set against a loss of, it may be,
£5,000.

Yet there are quite good plays, quite good performances, that only ten thousand people may want
to see, and cannot be hurried like sheep into seeing
(there are good books enough profitably produced
that not five thousand people can be expected to
read). But though they may want to see them, and
see them again and again—as one wants to re-hear
a Beethoven symphony, not every day for a week,
not every week for a month, but, say, two or three
times a year—and though in due time the ten
thousand might grow to be one hundred thousand
or more, under such conditions as these, if the

6

business man is to be really business-like, their taste cannot be considered at all. Where would our literature be if publishers were in like case? We should have the daily papers. Here, then, is one reason why private enterprise in the London theatre of to-day does not do for dramatic art all that it might.

Better aspects of the story may be found; but there are yet worse. The average London theatre cannot pay unless its stalls are fairly full. They cost not less than 10s. 6d. each, tax apart; and the terms of the lease keep them at that price. It may happen—it does happen—that the cheaper seats will be continuously full of people whose only fault is that they cannot afford more than 5s. for their entertainment. They may come in their crowds, and the play will still be a failure.*

Under such a system—so to call it—the wonder is not that private enterprise does no more that is creditable, but that it does so much; that, indeed, it does anything at all except try to gauge the passing fancy of the largest number of the stupidest people with the longest purses. Leave the art of the theatre out of the question, what is to be said even of a theatrical industry organised on such lines? There are one or two 'autonomous' managers remaining from an older order of things, who, conservative and experienced, contrive to remain. There are steady-headed business men who play a larger, riskier game, counting upon periodic large profits and cutting their losses quickly; but their relation to dramatic art is not, at best, much closer than the company promoter's to the industry he exploits; at the worst they are Stock Exchange gamblers in its shares.

* See Appendix 1, pages 120-121.

7

Escape from this cut-throat business has chiefly lain in the devotion of groups of enthusiasts, who have found their passive counterpart in rather larger groups of people, interested, some genuinely, some idly, some snobbishly, in art with a capital A, and willing to be cheaply entertained at odd times and in odd—often very odd—places. To the mass of gallant energy directed into this channel for the last thirty years we owe most of the fresh life that has been breathed into the English theatre, and the money-makers have found it a not unprofitable river in which to fish. But of what use is it to the average would-be playgoer, who has neither taste nor time for joining in these artistic conspiracies? Indeed, while one has little but praise for the producers and actors who, often at great sacrifice, will do work that interests them in this way rather than not do it at all, the audiences, with their we-are-for-the-latest-thing attitude (an attitude which masks more silliness than can be found in the frankest Philistinism), provide a deplorably unwholesome atmosphere, in which no honest art will flourish for long.

Moreover, while by this means good drama may be done, it simply cannot be done well. There are exceptions to this rule, of course, lucky chances by which play and company fit together, and the few hurried rehearsals that are possible produce surprising results. But the new thing and the good thing in drama are apt to present problems which ask some patience and care for their solving, and this cannot be looked for in time precariously snatched from the earning of bread-and-butter. Actors with reputations still to gain can run risks; actors with reputations to lose are to be forgiven if they do not choose to engage them in such hazards.

The ' side-show ' may make many interesting experiments; that is its function, and one which will always need to be fulfilled. But to expect it to provide us with catholic and mature dramatic art is to expect impossibilities.

We see what private enterprise does for the drama. It may come to do a little better or a little worse—it has, perhaps, done better before now —but I do not believe that those who are struggling with its difficulties will hold out hopes of its being able to do much more. It will always have its place in the theatre, and the largest place. There will be the actors, playwrights, and producers of very individualised talent, who will be convinced, and often rightly, that they can do better in full freedom. There will be the craving of a certain public for mere novelty to be appeased. There will be the appeal to the crowd, who are for the same dish as before with a slightly different sauce. There will be the small groups with unusual tastes. To make comparison with publishing again, private enterprise can be expected to provide the drama of journalism, of the popular novel, of the limited edition. But it cannot be looked to for a library of standard literature.

To provide this would be a large part of the function of the National Theatre. The parallel is not exact, of course. Fifty theatres, working at full pressure, could not compass the whole canon of the plays, old and new, that might claim a place. But a repertory theatre, containing two ' houses,' one large and one small, and with an adequate company, could stage from forty to fifty different plays in a year, and not one of them need be a poor one. It would, as a National Theatre, make all that is authentically Shakespeare its concern, not the

9

easily popular plays only, but the greater ones and the neglected ones. Eight or ten would be acted during the year, and each week should see at least two of them in the bill. The other Elizabethans would have occasional place, eighteenth-century comedy a more constant one. It would be easy enough to find every year a dozen or more plays written between 1880 and to-day, acclaimed in their time, acclaimed since, some of them as having come before their time—the generation that saw them would be glad to see them again, the generation that did not might find them worth seeing. For all the use they are now, without some such theatre as this to keep them in being, they might as well never have been written. There are foreign plays, too; half a dozen schools to pick from, each with its masterpieces. A National Theatre, however national, would no more neglect good foreign drama than will a public school to teach foreign languages or a university to study foreign literature. And if such a theatre could not find eight or ten new plays a year to produce—plays, whether farce or tragedy, written with integrity of purpose, not in catchpenny imitation of the latest success; that should be the test of them—the contemporary drama would be in a bad way indeed. What has the London play-goer, who wants to do his play-going under normal conditions, in reasonable comfort, and at moderate expense—what has he set before him now that can compare with this, what is he likely to have if things theatrical are to be left wholly at the mercy of the need to make as much money as possible in the shortest possible time?

The Repertory System

For that is a policy—as demoralising to good
business as to good art—which a repertory theatre,
a true repertory theatre, need never pursue. The
term ' repertory ' has, of late, been very loosely
used, and it is necessary to define it. A theatre with
a permanent company which produces a play and
runs it for a week or a fortnight, then drops it and
produces another, drops that in turn and produces
yet another, is not a repertory theatre at all. It may
do most creditable work. It will produce a satisfactory number of plays. The permanence of the
company makes their preparation simple and their
later revival—if they score an exceptional success
—sufficiently easy. But the restriction of a play's
run to the week or the fortnight is a serious draw-
back. For a failure this is not restriction enough;
yet the play must be acted to poor houses while the
next is prepared. And a success must be checked in
full tide. The slogging work is, moreover, a great
strain on the actors, who will, most of them, be un-
ceasingly rehearsing by day and playing by night.
And if some of them are left to stand more or less
idle for weeks at a time, this may be a yet greater
strain—upon patience and artistic morale. Such a
theatre is only by courtesy a repertory theatre;
it is actually a ' short run ' theatre. The system
serves to keep small towns and closely integrated
bodies of playgoers fed with theatrical fare which
would otherwise be denied them; but it is artistically unsatisfactory, and economically quite un-
suited to the huge amorphism called London.

The chief economic virtue of the true repertory
system is its elasticity; for a success can be exploited
and a failure limited to the fewest possible per-

formances. True repertory obtained in the old patent theatres (abolished in the eighteen-forties), and it obtains still in opera seasons, when the public finds no difficulty in grappling with its exigencies. In a repertory theatre no play is acted continuously. Four, five, or six different plays will be performed during a week (in a theatre with two ' houses,' double the number, perhaps). One play, if there is the call for it, may be given four performances in the week, another two or three, the rest a single performance each. This plan does not, of course, exploit the moment's success to the utmost (one hears the business man object). But if the public which could fill the house for eight performances have to be crowded into four and half of them crowded out, that (one puts it to the business man) at least does a play's reputation no harm; and the four performances a week can be continued throughout the year if need be, throughout the next year for that matter, and even after. The performances of the classics at the Comédie Française are probably past counting, but such a play as *Primerose* has had at the moment its 372, *La Marche Nuptiale* its 240; while at the Opéra Comique, if one may bring that into comparison, Charpentier's *Louise* has 756 to its credit; and there is *Carmen* with its 1,978. Reinhardt's Deutsches Theater in Berlin, with its Kammerspielhaus, was a privately endowed institution (never, probably, a profit-making one); in the autumn of 1910 his production of *A Midsummer Night's Dream* had been given over 500 performances there, and Bernard Shaw's *The Doctor's Dilemma* was, after two years, still attracting good audiences, and had been played 132 times.

But, if one must be a little thrifty with successes, failures, on the other hand, need not mean a succession of empty houses while a new play is prepared. The current repertory is announced a fortnight ahead (few people make their theatre engagements for more; this does not inconvenience the public) and need not be planned for more than three weeks. Thus no play need be booked for more than six or eight performances—if so many—before its fate is known; and few, it is to be hoped, would not be worthy of that much attention.

The present crude and artistically meaningless division between failure and success need not exist. Such a theatre would not be concerned with catchpenny productions. No play that had not some innate quality should find a place in it. Its more immediate public would come to have some faith in the management's judgment and be disposed to sample most of the dishes offered them; so that after awhile a minimum audience of a thousand or so could be counted on for almost any play. Then the problem is simply to adjust the further number of performances as exactly as possible to the larger public's demand.

Plays, like books, make every variety of appeal. There is the evergreen favourite, which may still not be everybody's favourite. Such a one, from the Shakespeare canon, is the *Merchant of Venice*, and a sympathetic *Hamlet* can always command an audience. Such a play is *The School for Scandal*. For the last twenty years there has been, with children, another—*Peter Pan*. Then there is the play which makes a quick brilliant success but exhausts its popularity as quickly; an old play, it may be, revivified by an arresting production, or a new play of topical interest. There is the play that is slow in coming to its own, of an attractiveness which ' grows on you,' that gathers its adherents by scores instead of hundreds, but keeps them. A discerning management of a repertory theatre could nurse many such a play to solid success. As things now are it perishes. Then there is the play that will never have more than a minority appeal. Yet it may be a very good play of its sort; and the unrepentant minority, in art as in politics, has its rights. The true repertory system, with its elasticity and its easily mobilised resources, can contain and profit by all these with their varying attractiveness, can profit by them financially when the present system must often lose by them, can always profit by them artistically.

The Neglected Art of Acting

With so much to do for the drama, there is still the service that a National Theatre could render to the art of acting, in giving the playgoer his good drama well done. There are those who say that the English *cannot* act, that the Latin races are your only actors. It would be waste of time to argue this. History contradicts it; but, whether or no, the English keep trying to act, are likely to keep on trying, are at their best when they are most English (very naturally, since acting must be the most spontaneously racial of all the arts), and at their worst when they emulate Latin methods—as the dramatists, who will try to write a sort of Anglo-French drama, the ' well-made ' play which the mid-nineteenth century made its standard—too often suborn them to do. Unless a nation has a robust resistant tradition of its own the influence of foreign drama and foreign acting (be it the best of its kind) can only be bad.

We have some good English actors to-day, as we always have had (the term is to imply actress too);

14

but as to any school of English acting, that is a very uncertain quantity. And as to tradition in the acting of Shakespeare or eighteenth-century comedy, it has vanished amid the present confusions. Not an unmixed evil, this. Shakespearean traditions had grown ever more and more vitiated, till it was high time for the actors to follow the scholars in at any rate a temporary return to the study of the Elizabethan stage. But small chance are they given to do that! It is hard to see how any school of English acting can arise in the anarchic conditions of to-day. Schools for would-be actors there are, excellent of their kind, no doubt. They teach the rudiments of the art, they must not pretend to do much more. But once he is launched on his career the actor is at the mercy of the market and its hazards. If he has luck, personality, and courage he will make something of a name for himself. And, having made it, what then?

The history of the English theatre for the past thirty years has from one point of view been the history of a succession of actors who, having made a reputation, have done little or nothing thereafter to fulfil it, have, in too many cases, sagged back into mediocrity, masking their impotence by an ever-increasing emphasis upon their popular manner, their successful tricks. Who can blame them? A man must earn a very high reputation indeed to have any effective choice of the plays he will act in; nor, for that matter, is an actor always very wise in his choice of plays—the actor-manager of the past was always apt either to let the actor in him betray the manager or the manager the actor. Successful actors, who nowadays must drift from theatre to theatre, have, at most, the choice between better parts and worse. Their line of continued success will be the line of least resistance; if they are paid their very considerable salary what can they expect besides? Now and then an unusual chance may occur. But it is their reputation that the business-minded manager pays for and needs for the strengthening of his play; the poorer the play is the more he needs it, so he will not experiment with it rashly. As for any of the really great acting opportunities, those that can turn a good actor into a great one, why should a manager go out of his way to provide them? Who will profit? The actor, and the next manager who engages him. So it comes about that we have this assortment of good actors who never get any better; and—really! —no great ones that we know of. It is not the young who lack chances; but the more mature, from whom more is expected, who are past the time for those rough-and-ready and artistically risky performances to which (quite rightly) the critics give such encouraging though, as it sometimes seems, such extravagant praise.

The acting of the past is notoriously far better than the acting of the present, and always has been. One must allow a little for that. Nevertheless—to take modern English comedy acting alone—will anyone pretend that the authoritative accomplishment of the acting of John Hare, of the Kendals, the Bancrofts, Ellen Terry, Mrs. John Wood, Charles Wyndham, Forbes Robertson, Arthur Cecil, Henry Kemble, Hawtrey, Beveridge, Waller, Calvert, Farren, Coghlan (one omits active survivors, and the list could be lengthened and lengthened) can easily, if at all, be matched to-day? Yet the actor of to-day is potentially every bit as good a man as his predecessors.

The group of actors who began their work in

the 'sixties and 'seventies of the last century had dramatic material to work upon which grew better all the time, which advanced in quality throughout the 'eighties and 'nineties with quite amazing strides. Few of them, it is true, took kindly to Ibsen and the then revolutionaries (and here, in breadth of interest, the present generation has the advantage of them; for those are now part of the accepted, if still too neglected, order of things), but they are to be excused for that. How should they not feel that the art of the dramatists, who had led them out of the puerilities and inanities of their professional youth, who had helped them make the English theatre a thing of some consideration again—how not feel that this art was, for them at any rate, all sufficing? Their own art had so matured in the light of it, and they and the dramatists (who had often been actors too) were unsurpassed taskmasters for the young: Sir Arthur Pinero, in particular, unsurpassed and unsurpassable. Drama of a narrow range it may have been; but let those who remember, for an instance, *The Gay Lord Quex* at the now demolished Globe Theatre (Kingsway traffic spins over the site) bear witness whether that was not, within its conventions, a fine accomplishment, and, in pure performance, finer, as a whole, than anything of the sort which may be seen to-day.

Finer as a whole! We have been speaking so far of individual actors, but acting is not an individual art. It attains full development—and this is particularly true of modern comedy—only in the complete accord of a whole company of actors. Nor can this accord be reached by the sudden throwing together for three weeks' rehearsal of even the most brilliant and generous individual talents. It comes with time and patience, variety of experience, and

17   C

the cultivation of a mutual sympathy which will be instinctive, not calculated. Once established (if one could express such things statistically), it doubles, and more than doubles, the artistic strength of a company. Some simulacrum of it is gained by the early training of actors in a set convention. In France, when the reputation of the Conservatoire was at its height and everyone was supposed to pass into the theatre by that gate, the most casually gathered company would at least find themselves working with a common method. It was a monotonous method unfortunately, too often method and nothing else, the thing that is falsely called ' style,' effect without cause. It gave grace to the good actor, but it enabled the bad actor to pass himself off as a good one. If we in England, in those days, had none of the advantages of Conservatoire training, we were not debauched by its vices either; our good actors were genuinely good, our bad actors (let alone) undisguisedly bad. It was a simulacrum, and no more, of the accord which belongs to a company working together in sympathy with a common aim, such a company as that—in its best days—of the Comédie Française, as those Brahm made famous at the Lessing, Reinhardt at the Deutsches Theater, such a one as the company led by the Poulsens and Frü Hennings at the Royal Theatre at Copenhagen, or as that inspired by Stanislawsky in Moscow.

It may be said that once the little group which worked under the Bancrofts for Robertson at the old Prince of Wales' had broken up (and it had not been, even so, an unchanging group), no such theatre existed in England. That is literally true. But the larger group which—with Pinero for a dominant dramatist—developed the Robertson-

18

Bancroft tradition through the eighteen-nineties were at least unanimous in their aims and methods. They did not work together in one theatre; if they had, there would have been a company ranking with the best in Europe. But there were not many of them, there were many links between them; and they disciplined new-comers to their particular creed, which did stand for something, integrate and achieve something. It had not the seed of survival in it (one could find reasons for that), but the memory of it stands in strong contrast to the lack of purpose, the fitful advances, the tacking to every wind of popular favour, the general extravagance and anarchy which rules in the theatre to-day.

The material now available in drama is far better, the material available for its acting is probably as good—why should it not be?—as ever it was. And the best of both is running to waste. A National Theatre would have its duty to the art of acting, and no casual one. It would give good actors great parts to play in surroundings that would enhance them; and we might—who knows?—see a little great acting again. One sometimes thinks that the older generation have forgotten—as it is evident, from their comments, that the younger generation do not know—what this is like. But have we no potential Othello or Lear or Oedipus, no Clytemnestra or Cleopatra who could stand up to stern criticism—and vanquish it? We have had them, and there is certainly no reason in nature that we should not have them again.

What is more, this ' accord,' which can transform a random collection of actors into a true company—even as a mob is made into a regiment—would, in turn, make of acting something that the average playgoer to-day never suspects it can be. Read the manuscript of one of the poorer plays of thirty years ago or so, some tenuous so-called comedy, remember the effect of its perform-ance, if it was one which Hare or Wyndham, Haw-trey or the Kendals dominated and inspired, and you will realise what the actor's art *can* contribute. Many an ambitious amateur of the time, anxious to shine in a London success, came suddenly to realise it (many, alack for their audiences, did not!) when the little orange-covered book came from Samuel French. Here, as he read, was the bare anatomy of a play; its quality had been the quality of its acting alone.

What good acting can do for a poor play it can do for a fine one. The task will not be so easy, nor its method quite the same—though at first all may seem a little easier, since the fine play will do something for itself. But quality in drama implies depth and complexity, though the finished surface may be smooth; and this it is that good and accordant acting will reveal and clarify. The finer the play the more it will gain. In modern drama the salient and now often quoted example of this transcendental power is in the story of Tchekov and *The Sea-gull*, which was given to a competent professional company, who treated it as they treated every other sort of play and—it could not be said to have died of the effect, for evidently it never came to life at all. Not till Stanislawsky and the nascent Moscow Art Theatre devoted themselves to discerning how Tchekov had to be acted was he found to be a dramatist. And, to the uninstructed, their acting came like the adding of the music to the libretto of an opera.

This may be an extreme instance of what this 'accord' can do. Buy why should it be? We do not know what can be done in this kind for the best of our own drama because we have never tried. We do know—and no actors who have had the experience but will confess it—the vital difference which even such cramped attempts at organisation as we have from time to time made can mean to the quality of their work. Nor is modern drama only in question. F. R. Benson and his company worked through the 'eighties and 'nineties of the last century under many limitations. Yet when, after ten or twelve years of something like stability, they came to London, he gave us Shakespeare done at least with a high spirit and consistent purpose which we have not seen approached since. Incidentally, his company then disintegrated. London managers were anxious to give all these apparently brilliant people better engagements—and how resist a London engagement?—and he had to begin all over again. But as individuals (it is no reproach to them) they did not all turn out to be quite so brilliant.

In conditions of security and stability such as Benson could only dream of what might not be done for the interpretation of Shakespeare? Some of his so-called lovers say they prefer to sit by their firesides to read him. What do they know of the alternative? If the Saxe-Meiningen company could make a German translation of Julius Cæsar a revelation to English playgoers fifty years ago, what might not an English company do—given the same chance, but it must have the same chance—for *Antony and Cleopatra*, *Othello* and *King Lear?* Not many of us prefer to sit at home and read the score of Beethoven's symphonies or finger them on the piano. We may prefer it, though, to hearing them scamped through by an orchestra recruited haphazard and given half a rehearsal under a conductor with his nose to his desk. But when Mengelberg brings his men from Amsterdam or Furtwängler his from Berlin we turn out on a rainy night and fight for our places.

The Audience

An instructive comparison, this. Such accomplishment and accord as informs a fine orchestra could in a company of actors make play-going a new thing. At present one goes—if one goes—to such and such a play, says after, " I've seen it "; and there's an end. You do not have music-lovers saying, "Oh yes I've heard the Ninth Symphony," as if that were a reason for not hearing it again. They go to hear it again and again, partly because it is a great work and appreciation of it grows with re-hearing, partly for the interest there is in fresh interpretations of it—which, indeed, help one to appreciate it more. People also go a dozen times to a good revue, not because of its intrinsic merits, but for the pleasure in the skill of the dancing and the fun. Only the drama, in nine cases out of ten, is left on a level with the newspaper which a man reads for information and throws aside, left with no one to care for the art of it, with an ever-diminishing public who even know in what the art of it lies.

In what the late nineteenth century used to call the ' palmy days ' of the drama, by which was meant the days of the Patent Theatres (National Theatres in their kind), this informed interest in the art of acting was very much alive. When Kean came to play Shylock and Hamlet and Othello, the critics and the public too were quick to note how his reading of this passage or that differed from Kemble's or Macklin's or Young's. We can read

22

Hazlitt and Lamb and Leigh Hunt on the subject still. Here was half the interest in the new-comer. It was a limited repertory played to a limited public, but they were amateurs of the art; even as nowadays we have our thousands of amateurs of boxing and football, cricket and golf and tennis, who will follow a game in full appreciation of its fine unexpected strokes. Kean's audiences at Drury Lane were not of the indifferent, acquiescent, 'amuse-me-if-you-can' temper of theatre audiences of to-day, but liker by far to the crowd in the centre court at Wimbledon when the finals are being played. They knew a masterly stroke when they saw one.

Good drama makes good audiences, and, in a very real sense, good audiences are in their turn the making of good actors. The contemporary drama of Kemble's and Kean's day was, with the rarest exceptions, pretentious and dull. But, in this respect, a repertory theatre's resources have multiplied out of knowledge during the last fifty years. There is Shakespeare still, and his contemporaries; there is still eighteenth-century comedy; and we have now on our shelves—which is not the exclusive place for it—a whole array of modern drama ranging from tragedy to farce, as remarkable a product as any renascent period of literature can show. We have the plays and the actors, and in London's millions, permanent and shifting, surely an audience. It is the organisation and a recognition of the need for it, that is lacking; this only.

A modern National Theatre's due dimension

Here then, generally speaking, is what such a theatre could be and do. In the chapters that follow will be found plans for its financing and working, full and accurate enough, I hope, for proof that it is an immediately feasible enterprise.

It will have to be a public enterprise; not in the sense that it need be run by the Government, but as the National Gallery and British Museum are, or as the lately established British Broadcasting Corporation is a public enterprise; or, in another category, as state-aided colleges and rate-aided schools, or as our older universities and public schools are, privately controlled in the public interest. The old sharp division in these matters has become blurred. We have devised—we have had to—more than one way in which such institutions can be given freedom from political interference, yet kept pledged to public service and sensitive to public opinion. There should be no great difficulty in drawing up a constitution.

There is, of course, no theoretical reason why private enterprise should not accomplish the task. But such a theatre must be, in more than one sense, a disinterested business. Quite apart from any question of profit, its fortunes cannot be let depend upon a personality or a group of enthusiasts. Artistic ' movements,' when their impulse is exhausted, are best dissolved; they have served their turn. But a theatre of this sort, with its need of an establishment and equipment, security and continuity of policy, must for good or ill be a permanent institution, and so organised. One would hope for the personalities and the enthusiasm for its service, and few things would matter more than to see that they were not smothered in routine. But they must exist for the theatre, not the theatre for them; it must survive when they are gone. Private enterprise could possibly create such an institution;

but to provide for its survival, it must inevitably be made a public trust of some sort.

Theoretically, again, the theatre might make profits; but in practice it almost certainly will not. It certainly cannot, if it is to be begun from the beginning upon a commercial basis, with, for a first charge, the earning of interest upon the large capital expenditure involved in the buying of a site, the building and equipping of the theatre, and the providing the repertory of the first three years with productions made, many of them, to last for at least nine. As we have seen, private enterprise in the theatre does not work along those lines. But, given its buildings and equipment and their bare upkeep, there is no reason whatever that a National Theatre should not balance its budget. The sensible thing would be to set it on the basis of a public school or university; not to expect it to pay interest on its foundation, but to cover its running expenses by its receipts. Here would be a rough-and-ready test of its efficiency, as useful to the management for a guide to the theatre's working as to the public for evidence that the trust was being fulfilled. And it could be said to be literally paying its way. If free performances, or some few very cheap performances are wanted, that will be another matter. It would be right to provide a special fund out of which they could be financed.

One thing more, before we pass from the general to a particular survey. *A National Theatre cannot be begun in a small way.* And anyone who thinks it can should be asked to work out the full implications of his heresy.*

Every enterprise has its fitting economic dimen-

* This, of course, does not rule out the need for adequate *preparation.* As to which, see p. 108.

sion; and enterprises, apparently of the same kind, may so differ in degree that the practical difference between them will be a difference in kind; the one can never grow into the other. A transatlantic liner and a Channel steamer are both passenger ships, but not only do their physical and economic dimensions differ, the whole scheme of their existence differs from A to Z.

One can compare this projected National Theatre to the ordinary London theatre in certain superficial ways. They must both employ actors to act plays for the entertainment of audiences. But the methods by which they will do it—in particular the economic methods, seventy-five per cent of them—will be too widely different for comparisons to count.

The scheme that follows can doubtless be advantageously amended in every detail. It might be possible or advisable to reduce a little, or increase, the numbers of the actors and the staff; reduce, or increase, the number of productions. But quite drastic reductions of this sort, it will be seen, would hardly lower expenditure by £20,000 a year—by less than ten per cent., that is to say, of the net expense, which receipts may be expected to cover. Administratively important questions these, once the theatre was in being, but not worth overmuch dispute now.

The main features of the scheme, on the other hand, are essential parts of its ' economic dimension '; the spacious and fully equipped building with its rehearsal rooms and scene studios and stores, a self-contained factory, in which between forty to fifty productions a year could be prepared or kept in being; the large and small auditorium and stage in which both more popular and less popular plays could each be economically acted, and the true repertory system that lets a play

26

be acted either as often or as seldom as there is call for it; the company numerous and well assorted enough for the casting of any play, and for the giving (in the two houses) of from eight hundred to nine hundred performances a year—upon *these* things both the artistic integrity and the finance of the scheme rests; and there can be no compromise, nor is there any half-way house to them. One is astonished to hear presumably instructed people exclaiming: " No bricks and mortar. A National Theatre Company by all means. The best plays, the best acting, but no vast unwieldy building." As well say to the Rolls-Royce Company: " Motor-cars, if you please, and the best of their kind. But no factory! " It comes of approaching the theatre by way of the front door. The work is done at the back; that is where the equipment is needed.

Such enterprises have their proper artistic dimension too. A National Theatre must do what ordinary theatres leave undone, and it must do things better than they do, or it will have but a sentimental justification for its existence—and *that* will not carry it very far. The competitive quality of its work must be sustained.

Also, it must do a great variety of work, for it must appeal to all sorts of people and to every sort of taste—except bad taste. Therefore the quantity of its output must be considerable.

A National Theatre must command attention, not apologetically beg for it. Adequately endowed and run upon generous lines, it can probably pay its way in a duly limited sense while it fulfils its task. Tinkered at, it will do neither. It will be a poor half-starved thing, shunned by the best dramatists and actors, and by the best of the public; or, to sustain it in respect, it will need extravagant subsidies.

27

CHAPTER II

THE CAPITAL COST

N o t the most careful calculation can give us this, here and now.

There is the question of the site. All one can say is that about so many thousand square feet will be needed in a suitable situation. What the cost would be must depend on the situation and upon a dozen other circumstances, impossible at the moment to foresee. One would hope not to have to buy it in the open market. The London County Council might surely take some share in providing it, might wish to do this much, at least, towards making such an addition to the amenities of the city they rule over. Can one see the city of Paris missing the chance? It must cost the ratepayers something (the Council does not own London), but less than it would bought competitively; and, even then, it need not be turned over as an unconditional gift. An actual site will be found suggested in the next chapter, which deals in detail with the theatre building.

The cost of the building and its equipment (though this, again, depends on the particular site) would be between £500,000 and £750,000, and probably nearer the larger figure. If this seems over-much for a building, note the 'and its equipment.' A National Theatre cannot consist, as other London theatres do, of an entrance, an auditorium, and a bare stage. It is to be a factory of productions; and its efficiency and the economy with which it can be run will largely depend upon the quality and

28

completeness of its equipment. But even as mere building cost this would not be excessive. There are two auditoria, two stages, workshops and scene-stores, rehearsal rooms and offices to be accounted for. The building of London's latest full-sized theatre, The Dominion, with its single auditorium and bare stage, has cost (site apart) £290,000.

There would need to be a fund of £200,000 to see the theatre through the first three years of its running; say £100,000 for the first year, and £50,000 each for the second and third. It is possible that this money would not all be sunk, as would be the money for the building (upon which interest in the form of rent could hardly be paid), and it might not all have to be called up. But the theatre must be made secure while it finds itself, determines and justifies its policy, gathers together its public; and a catchpenny policy for a start would be disastrous, doubtfully attractive to the fickle playgoer, certain to alienate the very people upon whose constant support and good word it should chiefly rely.

Out of this fund of £200,000 must also come the first capital expenditure upon productions. The detailed estimates which follow are drawn up for an average year, upon the assumption that the theatre has been ten years or so in existence. Forty-eight productions are supposed to be staged in such a year, but of these not more than ten might be new, and not all the material for these brand new.* The average ‘ life ’ of a production, reckoning in workmanship and material, is estimated to be four years. An average year would have, then, the fruits of former years to draw upon; but the first few years must see a large capital expenditure on this

* The cycle of Shakespeare Histories is reckoned, for the purposes of production, as three, not four plays.

account. There could, of course, be no attempt to reach the ' forty-eight production ' mark at a bound; the creation of the repertory and the furnishing of the scene and property stores will be a matter of time. This question and that of other preliminary work is considered in chapter xiv.

All this—the provision of the site apart—shows need for a sum of £950,000; if we allow £50,000 for errors of calculation we may call it £1,000,000. The money will not, of course, have to be paid into the bank in cash. Credit to this amount will be wanted. The two or three years that it would take to design and build the theatre would see the calling up of £750,000, and on this there could be no financial return. The rest might or might not have to be fully called up, and what was might or might not be recouped; a part of it possibly could be.* It may seem a large sum; but as capital expenditure upon an enterprise which, as we shall see, would have an annual budget of nearly £210,000, is it excessive?

A National Theatre not being a hospital, nor a scientific institution, nor out to provide the public with anything but spiritual benefit, the raising of £1,000,000 by private subscriptions would be a pretty formidable task. Nor with our traditions, and with the national finances as they now are and are likely to be for a generation, does one see a Chancellor of the Exchequer putting such an item nakedly into his budget. But, admit that the taxpayer could not be so plumply asked to provide the money, there is still a source available which is not —not precisely!—his poor overstrained pocket.

* The building up of the company of actors should be done while the theatre was building, and this also would need some financing. (See p. 108.)

The British Broadcasting Corporation has in three years become a handsomely profitable institution; most deservedly so, for its public-spirited policy has placed it head and shoulders above anything of its kind in the world. But if the British Government had not shown wisdom in giving it a charter and a monopoly, it could hardly be making these profits. As a set-off to its privileges, therefore, the Government retains (under a consequential agreement with the Post Office) twelve and a half per cent of each ten shillings which every possessor of a wireless set pays, or should pay, for a licence to listen-in; this for the expenses of collection (and the Post Office in 1928 recouped itself and made a profit of £17,745 besides out of the job). But, further, the Treasury retains another ten per cent in respect of the first million licences, another twenty per cent in respect of the second million, another thirty per cent in respect of the third million, and another forty per cent in respect of all in excess. The fourth million mark will probably, says the Postmaster-General, be reached very shortly; from that £500,000 alone no less than £262,500 (52½%) will be subtracted. Even upon the lower percentages the Treasury and the Post Office have not done badly; they will have gathered in just under £1,000,000 in the three years of the agreement's working (curious; just the sum the National Theatre needs for a credit).

Yet, in spite of all these deductions, the B.B.C. itself manages in its accounts for 1928 to carry down a balance of net revenue for the year of £123,181 4s. 1d. This in itself is thoroughly well-earned profit, and no one should want to interfere with it; improvements in an invention and a service still in its infancy may justifiably absorb it and its accretions for some while to come. But what about the pleasant £400,000 or so a year that the Treasury seems likely to inherit, as far as one can see, in permanence? This is not money wrung from the taxpayer; and no one, surely, will pretend that ten shillings is an exorbitant sum for a listening-in licence. Some of it then, at least, might be made available for the support of good drama—and here I add ' good music,' since in time there would be ample for both—for the rescuing of English culture in these arts from the imminent peril into which the Movie, the Talkie, the gramophone, and all the other contrivances for *re*producing rather than producing (for reproducing what will soon cease to be produced!) have elbowed it. Could not Conservatives, Liberals, and Labour agree to devote this money, before it becomes public money, while it is still the profit of this chartered monopoly, earned largely by the popularisation of these two very arts—to their salvation?*

The principle admitted, the simplest practical plan would probably be to rewrite Clause 18 of the 'Licence and Agreement' between the Postmaster-General and the British Broadcasting Corporation so as to vest the gross sum accruing from the listen-

* Mainly, it must be owned, by one of them. But the B.B.C. has already, more or less as a pure matter of business, done much for music. It cannot, for various technical reasons, do much directly for drama. Such an organisation as the National Theatre could, on the other hand, do some considerable service to the B.B.C. It could supply the personnel needed—yet not needed day in and day out—for the broadcasting of plays. It could work out the technique of broadcasting plays, a thing which still needs doing. And as this technique must largely consist in effective speech, there could be no better source from which to draw than a theatre for which this, with its classical repertory, would be a primary consideration. See also chapter xv.

32

ing-in licences (less a reasonable percentage—
twelve and a half per cent is high—for its collection) in Commissioners (who might well, with
small addition, be the Governors of the B.B.C.),
and empower them to spend it, first upon the maintenance and extension of the broadcasting service,
secondly upon the National Theatre, thirdly upon
a National Opera.* Thereafter the surplus could
be devoted to the assistance of municipal or other
disinterested enterprise in good drama and music
in other parts of the kingdom. During the last few
years the Carnegie Trustees have given much help
in this direction; but they will not, for they cannot,
continue to do so permanently. There are, both in
big cities and in villages, admirable enterprises of
the sort which may soon be faced with the prospect
of extinction. A few thousands a year would save
them.

There is much to be said against a settled permanent subsidy for theatres and opera-houses. The
management is encouraged to set it automatically
year by year upon the credit side of the balance-
sheet and then forget all about it. Far better to
envisage a proper balancing of takings and costs at
market rates. Then, if you have to, face the deficit—
which may be due to the carrying out of certain
public-spirited programmes, or to the paying
dearly for things of quality, or which may come
from selling these goods to the public, or to chosen
sections of the public, below cost price. It may be
policy to incur these apparent losses; all sorts of

* The friends of Opera will exclaim: Why not secondly? The
answer is both that Drama is the elder child, and can offer more
in return, a far richer and more varied product. Set the British
Opera already written in the scales against British Drama, and
Opera kicks the beam.

goods and services, judged necessary to the health of the bodies and minds of the public, are, in one way or another, retailed to it below cost price. But in such cases one should always know where one stands, and—if this is to be a public institution —the public should know. Therefore, if, its foundation apart, this theatre must have a subsidy (though as will be seen, except for the upkeep of its buildings this may by no means be necessary), let it be earned and deserved and justified, year by year.

Some of the surplus from the listening-in licences would first be needed as a credit for the building and launching of the theatre. Thereafter, if the money were made generally available, the Commissioners could be authorised to make yearly (or better perhaps over periods of three years) whatever grants could be afforded for the carrying out of approved programmes in this and other such institutions and enterprises. Their financial and artistic conduct would thus be kept under constant review, and revision if need be.

The system of " grants-in-aid " has on the whole proved to be a very good one. We need not turn for instances to the Board of Education and Local Government Board; here they have perhaps had to be standardised too much. But the Carnegie Trustees and King Edward's Hospital Fund have operated the system most successfully.

CHAPTER III

THE GOVERNMENT OF THE THEATRE

T H E British Broadcasting Corporation has five governors, and, under the charter, the number may be at any time increased by an Order in Council. The addition of four members, who had knowledge—not necessarily very expert knowledge—of dramatic and musical matters, would make this a very good body for the administering of the listening-in licence funds, and the theatre would need no other governing body.

The governors should control policy, and the power of the purse would give them ample power to do so. They might act as a court of appeal against any flagrant injustice; but, otherwise, *they should have no part whatever in the theatre's administration.*

They should appoint the general staff, to consist of—

> The Director,
> The Business Manager,

and (for reasons given hereafter)

> The Literary Manager, and
> A Reading-Committee man.

The Director would be their normal liaison with the theatre; and, having appointed him, they must let him direct. This is vital. He would attend them at the meetings at which they considered the theatre's business, every three months, six months, annually—as they thought best. He would then have to justify his past and advocate his future

35

policy. If they definitely disapproved of either, he would, of course, have either to conform to their views or resign. In the intervals he must be left free and responsible.

Surely one should not need to argue the point. A director of such an organisation—which would be a complex of conflicting interests, few of them to be expressed in terms of pure reason!—must have authority without having constantly to remind people that he possesses it. In a theatre, where everything depends upon mutual relations of confidence and sympathy, the indiscipline of unrest is demoralising to a degree; and conceive the unrest, if his less pleasing decisions, when he had to make them—and he would have to make decisions unpleasing to somebody about once a day—were not known to be the last word in the matter. Conceive the constant bringing of such matters before the Governors, or some advisory sub-committee. Think of the agendas for such meetings. Think of the Director having to argue each case all over again, with members who had been told this, or had heard that, had been distractingly lobbied in one interest or another. Will not the man have enough to do to manage his theatre without having to manage an ' advisory committee ' as well? No one with any experience of affairs, with any knowledge of the temperaments of dramatists and actors, would accept the post under such conditions, no man worth his salt would keep it if there were to be administrative questions he could not decide (" Wait till I meet my committee ") or after he had returned to the theatre a few times with his decisions reversed.

Freedom and its responsibility should be, if necessary, thrust on a Director. Once the laws of an organisation have been established and privileges and duties recognised, men and women like to serve under a man, who knows his own mind and decides the questions they cannot decide, gives them freedom to get on with their share of the work, nor leaves them hovering in doubt whether it may not be wasted. A Director who wanted the ' moral support ' of an advisory committee would not be fit for his post.

He would be ultimately responsible for the selecting and engaging of all the company and the staff, with the exception, as we see, of the three members of it (the rest of the so-called general staff) named above. There would, then, be certain limitations to his powers, and these are discussed in the next chapter.

CHAPTER IV

THE GENERAL STAFF

The Director	£4,500	a year
The Business Manager	2,500	,,
The Literary Manager	2,000	,,
The Reading-Committee man	750	,,
	£9,750	,,

N.B. With regard to the staff salaries and (in a lesser degree, for reasons that will be seen) the salaries of the actors, it must always be remembered that these estimates are not for a first year's working. They envisage the theatre fully established. For a first year there would need to be, as we saw, capital expenditure upon productions that would be no part of a normal annual account. It would, on the other hand, be specious to set down a first year's salaries as the last word in that matter. Length of service means increase of pay (a maximum in sight, of course); and, in an organisation with many departments and no great number of staff in each, this cannot often be set off against promotion. But a reasonable permanence of service there must be; no theatre of this sort could function with its staff in a constant state of flux. It is only fair, therefore, to put down figures that apply to an established concern.

These three first members of the general staff will be in control of a pretty large and complex organisation. Those that move in the world of ' big business ' and know the sums which good organising brains can command may say that they cannot be had at the price. Those that live in the world of literary and artistic enthusiasms will say they can be had for half the money. We may reply to the one objection that the best men will choose work they like in preference to more highly paid work which they don't; but to the other we must answer that mere enthusiasm plus the ability to make a very pleasant success in a small way will not give us men of the calibre needed for this sort of task. By recruiting from among simple enthusiasts, or the respectable unemployed, it would be perfectly possible to engage for less than half the sum a general staff who could be relied upon to make a mild or spectacular mess of the whole business and bring it to grief within three years—but that, after all, is not what we want.

The Director. A man of reputation and authority will be needed, of artistic knowledge, enterprising, and with administrative ability besides. Such men are rare, and in the world of the theatre—a world, in this region of it, of big rewards or none—they command their price. A very young man would not carry enough weight, nor too old a man have enough energy. Nor, in the future, would one be very likely to find the right man in the ranks of the staff or among the actors. It must always probably come to asking some outsider, in the full tide of success, to make material sacrifice for the honour and glory of the position. £4,500 a year, less income-tax, with the manifold expenses to be considered which such a position involves, and the disadvantageous relation to the pension fund*—all this taken into

* See Chapter VI.

39

account, the net income would be no more, certainly, than the work, well done, would be worth to the theatre; and much less, as certainly, than its equivalent could command in the open market.

The Business Manager is to receive £2,500 a year for the control of an expenditure of something like a quarter of a million. Efficiency in this post would be the only economy. In a theatre the fight against extravagance and waste is never finished. A good man would save the amount of his salary over and over again. First-rate financial brains are in any case not to be had cheap. The position, however, might be reached by promotion and the relation towards the pension fund be a better one.

The Business Manager, appointed by the Governors themselves, should be in direct relations with them; though, even so, not behind the Director's back. But they would often have to decide questions of policy on mainly financial grounds. They would need the expert's advice, and to be able to examine and cross-examine him personally.

The Literary Manager—the term is an awkward one—would take artistic control in the Director's absence. But his chief business would be with the texts of the classics, the quality of translations (he would need to be something of a linguist), and, most importantly, with the reading of new plays. With much more than their mere reading, however.

In the matter of plays—and there is no more vital matter—a theatre of this kind runs certain obvious risks. It is an important part of its duty, no doubt, to keep the classics in its bill and to see that other well-deserving plays are not forgotten. But here is the line of least resistance, and by pursuing it too exclusively, the theatre would soon dig itself deep into a rut of dull routine. On the other hand there will come crowding in all the manuscripts which the theatre of private enterprise has rejected, this alone seeming to the authors ample reason for the National Theatre to accept them. The theatre of private enterprise complains from time to time that it cannot get good plays—by which, however, it mainly means good plays which will run for three hundred nights. The fact is that good plays, like other good things, need cultivating. Dramatists need to be encouraged to write them. This Literary Manager, then, would not have to be a man who sat in his office and read what came to him; he would need to be out and about, seeing new plays at home and abroad, and to be, above all, in sympathetic personal relationship with dramatists—of the younger school as well as of the old. Upon his personality and critical flair would depend the freedom of the theatre from the reproach which is apt—and quite unnecessarily —to fall upon all academies of being behind the times.

In this one matter alone, the choice of plays, sole responsibility should not rest with the Director. To begin with, no one man, occupied as fully as he must be, could possibly deal fairly with the mass of manuscripts or hope to see all the new productions of potential interest elsewhere. Again, no one man's taste is likely to be catholic enough, nor his apprehension of the unexpected (the new thing in drama lies close hid in a mere manuscript and may well escape all but the keenest eye) sufficiently alert. Two men's outlook even, especially when the theatre, as it must, bulks largely in their daily life, would probably not be wide enough. For that reason, when William Archer

41

and I first drafted this scheme, we proposed to add yet a third to the play-council, the Reading-Committee man, and I still think the suggestion sound. Someone to bring to it as divergent a point of view as possible, who should himself be—and keep—removed from the daily life and interests of the theatre. The work would not ask all his time. He would not have to wade through the bulk of the manuscripts, though he might well bring some for consideration on his own account. One sees a man of letters in the post, sympathetic to the drama, of course; a critic, perhaps, but not necessarily or even advisably a dramatic critic. Nor, I now think, should the appointment be a permanent one. Its object would obviously be better served if the divergent current of ideas were drawn from a fresh source every three years or so.

It would be possible, of course, to make these two merely advisers to the Director. But advice, with no further responsibility attached, is seldom over carefully given. There is more to be said for allowing the Director at least a suspensive veto upon the production of any play, which he thought he could not, for reasons of casting or the like, satisfactorily add to his repertory at the moment. In this one matter alone—which is not, be it noted, a matter of administration, until the choice of a play is made—three heads would probably be better than one, and they should find no real difficulty in resolving their properly discordant opinions into harmony. One thing is certain: upon a catholic and enlightened choice of new plays the best fortunes of the theatre would depend.

CHAPTER V

THE SITE AND THE BUILDING

I N what shape the improvement scheme will finally leave it cannot, at the moment of writing, be told, but the site facing the river between the County Hall and the Surrey approach to the new Charing Cross Bridge is about all that one could wish for; a National Theatre could hardly be better placed. And if the new station is not to hug the river on the other side of the approach, a National Opera House could find a place opposite. A mass of Londoners—and, what is perhaps more important, of strangers—would be reminded daily of their existence. They would stand there as salient evidence that, at long last, a reproach to our civilisation had been removed. The picturesque aspect of the site does not need stressing, but its practical advantages are many. Its cost—to the London County Council—if it were now set aside for the purpose would not be extraordinary. There is ample space; the theatre, with all its offices and work rooms, could be built as a self-contained unit, and this alone would mean a saving in running expenses of thousands of pounds a year. No other such site in any such central position is likely to fall vacant within a generation or so. This will become, in accessibility, one of the chief centres of London. For a last recommendation, it should be possible to connect the theatre by sub-way with Waterloo and Charing Cross stations, as well as with the various tubes; and there is the worst of that most difficult problem of winter theatre-going in London—the problem of transport in bad weather—solved for a few millions of suburban inhabitants, season-ticket holders many of them, who can reach a railway terminus easily and cheaply enough, but who now think more than twice about the chances and cost of cabs on a rainy night.

Is it too much to ask the London County Council to make this site their contribution to the adding of such an amenity—such an ultimately very profitable amenity in its attractiveness to strangers—as the National Theatre will be to the city whose interests they serve?

As to the building, it is hard to be particular about it apart from a site. Yet its practical particularities are what matter, and it was with a view of getting these defined that the British Drama League, some years ago, fathered a competition for a design; an excellent if unobtainable site being indicated, since some site had to be; South Square, Regent's Park. This was won by Mr. W. L. Somerville of Toronto, and won largely because of the attention he gave to the details of the theatre's practical needs.

For such a theatre must not be thought of—the layman naturally thinks of any theatre so—as an auditorium and a stage, behind which, in some dark mysterious corners, the actors lurk between times. The stage is the shop counter upon which the finished product is displayed. But a repertory theatre—this repertory theatre, at any rate—has to be, as we said, a factory in which it will be possible to prepare and present, with the utmost economy of money, time, and strain upon the human material employed, some fifty different plays a year.

44

And the layman, if he wishes to know why it will be wise to spend £750,000, or more, upon the building and equipping of such a factory, must give at least a cursory glance at the problems involved.

The need for the two auditoria—or 'houses' as it will be more convenient to call them—is fundamental, artistically and economically too. In point of size, one house would have to be a compromise. It could not be exactly suited both to the *Agamemnon* and the comedies of Mr. Milne and of Hubert Henry Davies. Nor could it be big enough for the due exploiting of a popular success, yet not too big for the audiences which a more select play might draw. But this theatre must do all sorts of plays and at the same time keep up a high average of receipts. When it can legitimately draw crowds it must, and plays which might barely half fill a large house could not be let constantly exclude plays which would quite fill it. Moreover—as we shall see when we come to consider the size of the company that will be needed for the due filling of lengthy casts— with one stage only available, for half the time more than half of them might be standing idle while plays with small casts were acted. One house, in fact, would artistically give no play its best chance and economically would mean waste both ways, in the paying of actors for doing nothing and in the waste of empty seats which might be filled.

The two houses must be under one roof, because this makes the use upon either stage, sometimes of the same scenery, more frequently of the same furniture, properties and costumes, a practicable matter. You cannot be always carting these things about. It costs a great deal of money; moreover, it ruins them. This theatre must look to keep its best productions in being for years, and the cost of their upkeep should never be more than ten per cent. This will be impossible if the material of them— some of it very fragile—is to be harshly handled. For the same reason there must be ample store-room (with machinery for the conveyance to and fro of scenery and furniture), a carpenter's shop and a paint frame. Mr. Somerville's provision for this is simple and excellent. The scenery is lowered to the cellar (a deep cellar, costly to excavate, but of paramount necessity; it must give clearance to the scenery) and thence taken by electric trolley to the stores (or shops) in the centre section of the building. Similar arrangements could be made for taking furniture to the roof and making its store there. Furniture and scenery should never be jumbled together.

Coming to the general plan of the building: the two ' houses ' must be as far apart as possible, sound proof, one from the other; for it will not do to have the scene by the fountain in *Pelleas and Melisande* interrupted by the shouts of the crowd in *Julius Cæsar*. The centre section of the building, intervening between the two, provides well for this. Moreover, something of the sort, in at least semi-isolation, will be a necessity; for the County Council's fire regulations do not permit the storing of more than a production or so at a time in any theatre. Nor will their building regulations allow the placing of one house above (more or less) another, as the two houses of the Théâtre des Champs Elysées in Paris are placed (not but that this is inconvenient to the last degree). So, by every consideration, we are driven to a large ground plan, as we are also, of course (by building regulations again), driven to a site isolated upon at least three sides. This alone must make the building costly.

46

The centre section also contains the chief rehearsal rooms; they are thus as sound proof in relation to the two houses as, probably, it will be practicable to make them; not perfectly, but the noise made here can always be kept under control. Mr. Somerville allows five altogether, large and small, and this would be none too many. Here, again, is a question of economy. It costs money to rehearse on a stage: directly in the employment of light and labour, indirectly in the postponement of other work that has to be done there, till this is being done in ' overtime '—the curse of every economical stage manager. In a repertory theatre with its constant change of bill there is always scenic work to be done on the stage. Only dress and scene rehearsals could properly take place there as a rule; a play's preparation would have to be brought to that point in the rehearsal rooms. Yet a mere ordinary room, as everyone knows, is of no use for this purpose; a stage of full working size is needed and a pretence of an auditorium from which a producer can focus the effect of the acting.* These also must be under the one roof. For here another and as important an economy is involved; economy of effort for the actors. In the ordinary London theatres of to-day rehearsals are a three or four weeks' spasm of violent and distracted activity; with the run of the play—if there is a run—comes routine. It will be far otherwise in this theatre. There will be as many performances, and more; but no one actor will be taking part in all of them; if in two-thirds it will be much. But he will be steadily rehearsing, more steadily in every sense than now. Upon some days he may have to pass

* By working size is meant the area the acting occupies, which is usually, of course, a tithe of the full stage.

47

quickly from rehearsal to performance; sometimes he will be only rehearsing, or performing only. His daily professional life will be centred in the theatre, as another man's is at his office; and if his energies are to be kept fresh, it must be physically centred there. The senior members of the company will have their properly furnished dressing-rooms— each his own—which will equally serve for study or rest, and from them they must be able to pass easily to stage, rehearsal room or wardrobe.* This will not seem a trivial matter to those who have ever been involved in the distractions of a big pro- duction, with rehearsals being held and costumes made here, there, and everywhere at once. From an occasional debauch of the sort its victims recover easily enough; but week in and week out indulgence in it would soon bring the hardiest company to ruin.

The foyer common to both houses is an excellent feature. One could hope to have inter-act music there, and so induce people to leave the auditorium for ten minutes to be aired. The tea-rooms, grill, and refreshment bar: these are not only conveniences but would be sources of profit to the theatre. Almost all London theatres to-day lack space for them.

The Library. Without one no National Theatre would be complete. The literature of dramatic art grows yearly in bulk and importance. Where better could it be studied? Besides this, as the years pass, the records of the theatre, its prompt books and designs, will become of value. They must be avail- able to students.† A lecture room will be needed,

* Mr. Somerville's arrangement of the dressing-rooms, and of that part of the theatre in general, is not altogether happy. But this is a minor problem of planning.

† The Opera House in Paris has, of course, a very valuable library. So has the Théâtre Français; and most other old established State Theatres must have them. William Archer's

and the library could serve for this. And it would be the place in which upon occasion the theatre could welcome dramatists, critics, and distinguished men and women of the theatre from other lands.

As to the two houses themselves: the larger should hold from eighteen hundred to nineteen hundred, the smaller round about one thousand. Mr. Somerville adopts what is often called the 'Bayreuth' plan; it is, of course, a modification of the Greek theatre. This is excellent up to a point. No one sits with heads—or hats—interrupting his view, or with the ceiling of the balcony above impending on him and robbing him of air. But—in the larger house at any rate—it may set the furthest spectators too far from the stage. Admit one not too deep gallery at the back, even two, and this difficulty is solved.

There are three things to avoid in an auditorium, and Mr. Somerville has avoided all three.

People in a theatre should never be regimented in straight rows. The seating ought always to be upon the arc of a moderate sized circle. This keeps them in touch with each other as well as with the stage, makes a friendlier assemblage, and makes it far easier for the actors—let the psychologist explain why—to create and sustain an 'emotional atmosphere.'

The various categories of seats must not be unalterably divided. This is the objection to a many-galleried house. You cannot easily bring the two empty rows of a 7s. 6d. gallery to the relief and profit of an over-crowded 5s. gallery. London theatres now shift their pit barriers, often from performance to performance, and so add to or

theatrical library is actually waiting in the care of the British Drama League, to be presented to the National Theatre.

49   E

diminish their stalls. But this, carried too far, becomes a vexatious practice. No play-goer likes to
find himself paying 10s. 6d. upon one evening for
a position in a theatre which two weeks before cost
him only 3s. If the difference is between 10s. 6d.
and 7s. 6d., he will not object so much. Besides, in
a long-run theatre we go to see a particular play
and may not enter it again for a year; but with a
repertory theatre, constantly changing its bill, it is
the theatre itself that we get into the habit of visit-
ing, and these things would count. It will be well
to provide for as much elasticity as possible in this
matter—since each play tends to develop a drawing
capacity of its own, and the theatre's aim must
always be to accommodate itself to this as exactly
as possible—and for an even gradation in the advantage and value of the seats.

The third thing to avoid is, very simply, discom-
fort. There is no reason whatever that theatre-
going should be a physical penance. The number
of middle-aged and elderly people who are kept
from the theatre nowadays, and particularly from
the cheaper seats, because they will not face this—
not to mention the risk of its being an æsthetic
penance as well—is large and increasing. One of
the aims of a National Theatre must be to make
theatre-going a habit for intelligent adults. It must
cater for them spiritually and physically too.

Much will depend on the ingenuity of the architect. The main demand upon him is for a large
house, which will not be too large for the broad
playing of modern comedy and a small house which
will not look empty with no more than 600 people
in it. It should easily be possible to fulfil this condition with the small house, and give it, at the same
time, a capacity of 1,000 or rather more; this is

enough for the exploiting of a success, while the sight of an audience of 600 in it will not cry out failure. But in sizing up the large house one must be more careful, and must be especially careful in comparing any plan for it with existing theatres, with the older ones above all, for each has its idiosyncrasies, and in many of them the published 'capacity' figures include some impossibly bad seats.

The Comédie Française is supposed to hold 1,400. It is over lofty but not too large for the playing of comedy. It is 'old-fashioned' in its planning, and has the virtues of this. Without much apparent enlarging, it could probably be replanned to hold another 200. The Odéon only holds 1,250. It is wastefully planned.

The Paris Grand Opera, to one's surprise, only holds 2,200; but it has tier upon tier of boxes. No one could play comedy there. The Opéra-Comique, in which one just could, only holds 1,500.

The Théâtre des Champs Élysées boasts of 2,200 places. It is certainly a vain boast. But it probably contains 1,800 to 1,900 good seats. It is, but for some overplus of boxes, admirably planned, and is hardly too large for comedy playing.

Of the London theatres: no one would want to play—or see—comedy in the present Drury Lane, which has about 1,260 reserved seats, not counting its boxes, and probably another 1,000 unreserved.

His Majesty's has nearly 1,000 reserved seats, possibly another 800 unreserved. This is amply large, but—a little differently planned—just not too large.

The Palace (the old English Opera House) may be a little larger.

The Haymarket holds something under 1,000

people; an excellent house for comedy. The small house in the National Theatre should be just about this size. The St. Martin's Theatre holds at most 612; it could not be so small as that.

For other foreign theatres: the Burg Theater at Vienna has 1,474 seats; the theatre at Prague 1,800; the National Theatre at Oslo 1,400.*

Clever planning, then, it seems, could give us a large house with a capacity of 1,800 to 1,900; but no more, if it were to be fit for the playing of comedy —as it must be. For the smaller house one should aim at 1,000 to 1,100.†

Mr. Somerville's stages are excellently—perhaps excessively—capacious. The larger is 135 ft. wide by 80 ft. deep, with a proscenium opening of 44 ft. Full wide an opening, but a movable proscenium reduces it. The smaller measures 135 ft. by 64 ft. with a proscenium opening of 30 ft. There is ample sideroom; and this is *the* important thing for the shifting of scenery. Some of the depth could be spared. An apron stage and a Greek " orchestra " are provided for. The need for these—for the apron stage in particular when Shakespeare is in question —will, one hopes, no longer be disputed. But they must be provided for in the original planning of the house, since all the lines of sight are involved.

* Or had twenty-five years ago. I take these figures from the *Scheme and Estimates.*

† Mr. H. M. Harwood suggests (see p. 124) that a third house, a " studio," holding a couple of hundred people, with a stage accommodating only the simplest scenery, might be provided for student performances and for very experimental plays. This—if space could be found—would be an excellent addition (it could also be used as a rehearsal room); but as its working would probably show neither profit nor loss, it will be better, at the moment, to leave it, and the minor complications it suggests, out of account.

CHAPTER VI
THE COMPANY

Inclusive yearly salaries £75,200

Actors:					
2	at	£2,500	a year	£5,000	
2	,,	£2,000	,,	£4,000	
2	,,	£1,750	,,	£3,500	
4	,,	£1,500	,,	£6,000	Paid in
4	,,	£1,000	,,	£4,000	salaries and
4	,,	£750	,,	£3,000	fees
8	,,	£600	,,	£4,800	
15	,,	£500	,,	£7,500	
15	,,	£400	,,	£6,000	
15	,,	£250	,,	£3,750	Salaries only
71				£47,550	

Actresses:					
2	at	£2,500	a year	£5,000	
1	,,	£2,000	,,	£2,000	
1	,,	£1,750	,,	£1,750	
1	,,	£1,500	,,	£1,500	Paid in
1	,,	£1,000	,,	£1,000	salaries and
6	,,	£750	,,	£4,500	fees
6	,,	£500	,,	£3,000	
6	,,	£400	,,	£2,400	
6	,,	£250	,,	£1,500	Salaries only
30				£22,650	

Producers : 3 at £1,000* a year   £3,000 Salaries only

Supers and the expenses of students
" walking on "   £2,000

Actors	£47,550
Actresses	£22,650
Producers' salaries	£3,000
Supering	£2,000
	£75,200

* The salaries would be supplemented by a fee for each production, which it is more convenient to include in production expenses. Some actors in the company would also undertake the production of plays in which they did not appear.

53

Here we have a company of seventy-one actors and thirty actresses all told, from which to cast, say, fifty plays in a year of fifty-two weeks and (in the two houses) eight hundred and eighty performances.

At no one moment, however, will the company be at this full strength. There is illness to be considered, and each actor will need four weeks' vacation or more.* We must make a deduction of at least ten per cent on this account. The strength of the company at any given moment will then be: sixty-three actors, twenty-seven actresses.

The great disproportion between actors and actresses is, of course, determined by the amount of Shakespeare that has to be played. Men, in his casts, will often outnumber women by eight to one. The disproportion lessens through the eighteenth century, but even in modern plays it is—for some reason—seldom adjusted to nature.

The total number of the company depends, not only on the number of plays, but the number of performances to be given. It is clearly good sense to keep an expensive establishment open to custom for as many hours as possible. With one play in the bill there will be the question of how many performances of it the public will absorb; but not with a variety of plays. The limit then will rather be the capacity of the two stages for performances and necessary rehearsals. It should at times be possible to give twelve performances a week; even with new productions and their dress rehearsals supervening, it should never be really necessary— the staff being efficient and well used to the work —to drop below eight. But we had better allow for

* ' Actor,' except when the context contradicts, is to include ' actress.'

the emergency of a pressure of rehearsal work and for certain summer weeks, unfavourable to matinées, and, for our calculations, reduce the potential 934 performances to 880; 440 in each house.*

The number of the company also depends, of course, upon the impossibility of the actors, even of small parts, rehearsing daily and playing eight or nine times a week all the year round. Nobody should be in more than six performances a week, and actors of important parts not in more than four or five. The ' eight performances a week ' custom is comparatively new; and it is one, at least, of the causes of the decline of quality in modern acting. It is bound to lead to automatism. It has a particularly disastrous effect upon the younger actors playing the smaller parts (and just at the time when they are most impressionable). With the best will in the world they cannot give variety— eight times a week!—to their thirty or forty lines. And even the long parts fall into mechanical repetition; spontaneity becomes trick, however cleverly disguised. As to great parts; no man can *act* Hamlet or Othello or Macbeth eight times a week. He would kill himself within a month if he tried to.

* The figure 934 allows for Christmas Day's and Good Friday's closing. And it is worth while noting that, if ever Sunday performances are legalised, the objection—a real objection—of the seven-day week need not apply to this theatre. The only extra expense involved, besides light and heat and such items, would be a supplementing of the staff; but not of the company, probably, nor of the heads of departments.

For the sake of simplicity of statement, one must, in a book of this sort, calculate by averages. The probability is that there would be more performances in the large house than in the small, for cheap popular performances could be more profitably organised there. The financial aspect of this is discussed in chapter xi; we are now only concerned with the working capacity of the company.

Garrick, Kemble, and Macready would have been shocked at the notion. An actor may *act* the whole part through, say, once a week, to remind himself that he can; for the rest, he can only act a scene or two on one night, another scene or two on another; he repeats the rest by rote, however cleverly he may disguise the fact. It will, indeed, be far better for his art to repeat well than to act badly, forcing the combination of thought and emotion which makes true acting when he cannot happily achieve it. But acting is what we go to the theatre to see, and, at eight repetitions a week, we can seldom get it. Therefore, ever seldomer do some of us go.

The number of the company yet further depends upon two considerations which the theatre will ignore at its peril. There must be no play in the normal category of plays which cannot be played because it cannot be cast. *King Lear*, for an instance, cannot be long left out of the bill for lack of a Lear, or *Antony and Cleopatra* for lack of a Cleopatra. And there must be none of that playing of ' lines ' of parts (First Old Man, Second Old Woman, Singing Chambermaid!) which was the curse—and at last the doom—of the old stock companies. Nor, when it comes to modern plays, can there be a necessitous thrusting of square pegs into round holes. The modern author must have a reasonably wide field of choice for the casting of his play, or he will not bring it to the theatre. Full freedom he cannot have; if in theory he has it now, in practice it is largely illusory; the coherence and better general quality of the company should be full compensation for small loss.

The Need for Two Stages

Nor, were there one stage to play upon instead of two, could the number of the company be very greatly reduced. Since this may seem a very obvious economy to make, let us look into the fallacy of it with some care.

With one stage only, a representative repertory of plays would still ask for a company of not less than sixty-six. That at least is the figure which William Archer and I arrived at when we drew up our *Scheme and Estimates*. We went into the matter very thoroughly, casting every play in the year's list of productions, with each play's needs and with actual individual actors in mind; and forty-two men and twenty-four women were needed for adequate casting. See now what might well happen, with one stage only to play upon. In the specimen repertory set down in chapter vii. there are *Antony and Cleopatra* and *Henry V*. There is also *Peer Gynt*. The first will absorb thirty-four men and four women, the second about forty men and four women (some parts can be doubled, but too much doubling is an undesirable sort of thrift), and the third something like thirty men and twenty women. There is also Flecker's *Hassan*. And if we happened to be considering *Cyrano de Bergerac*, here are forty-two parts for men and thirteen for women. These, and plays which make like demands, must be acted, and the company must be measured to their needs. But they might in any year be acted for comparatively few performances, and the successes might be such plays as *The Importance of Being Earnest* (with its cast of nine) or even *The Mollusc* (with its cast of four). These, certainly, are extreme instances; but even the normal chances of an extended repertory

57

must, it is easy to see, keep far too many actors standing idle if there is only one stage upon which they can be acting. I turn back to the *Scheme and Estimates* to find that in its season of forty-six weeks no actor played more than one hundred and sixty-nine times and no actress more than one hundred and six (except the players of quite small parts). That is well enough if they are constantly rehearsing too. But one actress only played forty-one times and several others less than seventy times; one actor only seventy-two times and nine of them less than one hundred. This was a serious flaw in the scheme; none the less because the lower scale of salaries of those days enabled one to overlook the waste of money involved.

The standing idle should not have been overlooked. Good actors will not stand idle, even if they are paid to. And the waste of money we now cannot overlook. Turn this two-house estimate into a one-house estimate, reduce the company by a third (this, without calculation to that end, turns out to be the exact difference between the needs of one house according to the old *Scheme and Estimates* and the two as now presented) and the waste in salaries paid to actors left standing idle for lack of a second stage would be something like £46,000 a year. That, clearly, is intolerable; and the provision of two houses, by which the margin of idleness can be reduced to as near vanishing point as possible, is the obvious, is really the only remedy. There is none in the employment of actors who do not care if they stand idle and will do it cheaply, or whom nobody else will employ; this would be reduction in quality. Nor is there in the anarchy of a company with half its members for half the time occupied elsewhere.

The actor's work is of course not to be thought

of wholly in terms of performances; the study and preparation of plays (something more comprehensive than mere rehearsing) and, as importantly, the keeping of the current repertory fresh and interesting will be as predominant a part of it. With everything reckoned in there should be very little standing idle. At times the plays in both houses might happen to have small casts; at times a little contriving would be needed to prevent plays with large casts clashing. But, in general, the flow of work should be fairly steady, and the margin of unemployment a narrow one.

The Fee System

The actors' earnings are here set down, for the sake of simplicity, in round figures, but in practice they would accrue upon a system of salary plus fees and be subject to some slight variation.

The system suggested is this. An actor would be engaged for a period of three years, with the understanding on both sides that, all being well, the engagement would be renewed; for the general permanence of the company is a basic necessity. From a third to half his earnings would come to him in the form of a fixed salary. For the rest he would be paid a fee for each performance he gave, and a certain number would be guaranteed to him. In a lucky year—or, let us say, for a year in which he had contributed to make several productions a success—his income would rise; it could never fall below the guaranteed minimum; if the management had not employed him to that extent, it would be the management's loss.

The system has many advantages, which are set out at length in the *Scheme and Estimates*. To recapitulate them shortly:

It helps counteract the tendency to slackness which may beset the most conscientious of us once we are in financial security. The more useful an actor proves himself, the more he will be in demand and the higher his income will rise above the guarantee.

It enables the management to adjust and re-adjust an actor's earnings to his utility to the theatre with the least possible friction. For instance, upon each renewal of an engagement the salary paid should increase until a recognised maximum was reached (it should at any rate never decrease). This is the universal rule in stable institutions that encourage long service. But the amount of the fee and the number of performances to be guaranteed could be adjusted to the actor's immediate usefulness. The generally useful actor would tend to earn a small fee and to have a large number of performances guaranteed him. For the actor of great value in particular parts it would be just the other way. With an ageing actor both fees and number of performances might have to be diminished; but he would always keep his basic salary, and, with this, his position of seniority in the theatre.

The system automatically limits the Director's theoretical power (which he must have) to cast any actor for any part without question. The notion that a man should play Hamlet on one night and a footman the next, just to show that this is a repertory theatre with high artistic aims, is an absurd one. But an actor would be protected from anything of the sort by the fact that no sane management would go on paying, say, £5 a performance for the playing of a part which could be equally well played for £1.

Lastly, the amount of an actor's retiring pension could best be calculated upon the basis of a fixed salary, and for this reason alone the salary must not be liable to diminution (as it would have to be if it were his total earnings, and his value to the theatre diminished). He could not be allowed to profit by leaving the theatre when his earnings were at their highest, long before he was of a pensionable age. This would create an unfair charge upon the Pension Fund. But a man must be free to leave (and, more importantly, the Director must be able to get rid of him) without forfeiture of the pension he has legitimately earned.

The Pension Fund

A pension fund is an integral part of these calculations. The detailed plan of one will be found worked out in the *Scheme and Estimates*. Not the actors only will come into its benefit, but all the permanent staff of the theatre, and this must be constantly kept in mind in considering the salaries allotted to them.* It will not be created by deductions from salaries but by setting aside ten per cent from the takings of all non-copyright plays. This should build it up, under these new conditions, at the rate of from £6,000 to £7,000 a year; and by the time pensions began to fall due—for actors, it is suggested, if they choose to retire, or if they are compulsorily retired, at the age of sixty, for actresses at fifty-five—there should be a fund sufficient to provide them upon a very satisfactory scale.

This would certainly be an added attraction to the service of the theatre, and an inducement to remain faithful to it; an attraction, at any rate, to

* Those, it is suggested, whose engagements are upon the three-year basis.

61

the sort of actors—to the sort of men and women—
that the theatre would most want to attract. It
would be a future compensation for the loss of
those immediate opportunities for profit which
come with a sudden success, which must naturally
tempt a man to leave an institution offering well-
paid security only. Yet another set-off against such
loss will be referred to a little later. But actors with
whom a variety of interesting work and some dignity and security of position count for nothing at
all, will not, in any case, be in place in this National
Theatre.

Market Rates

As to the actual sums set down, it will be well to
explain how they have been arrived at.

To begin with, seven of the plays in the repertory were fully cast from among a company of
twenty-five men and fifteen women, authentic
actors of reputation and proved ability, neither
'stars' nor beginners. Leading parts were allotted
to those who had already played them, and the
usual weekly salaries earned were set against the
names. Then the average amount of employment
that each of these actors would have in a year was
estimated, and on this basis a likely salary for a
three years' engagement was fixed. With the pension fund and other special advantages the theatre
could offer in mind, these salaries were again reduced by from fifteen to thirty per cent, the proportion varying with the difficulty there might be
in replacing the actor by another who would possibly prove as good. Then other plays were considered
—plays which it would be the obvious duty of the
theatre to stage—containing parts which none of
these actors could fill; and something of the same

process was gone through with the known or surmised salaries of actual actors who could fill them. Then the necessary number of actors for the whole repertory was considered.

This still left the salary list at a very large sum total indeed. But, upon analysis, two or three things became clear. First, that it would of course be easy, with the opportunities the theatre had to offer, to recruit young actors for the smaller parts. It is proposed, as a glance at the bottom of the lists will show, to establish a ' moral minimum ' of £250 a year. A young actor who has had his training (and the theatre would hardly employ anyone who had not) is either worth this or nothing at all.* Incidentally, these are one-year, probationary engagements.

Secondly, one saw that the middle ranks of the company could be filled without much difficulty upon fair terms. No actor in this category is quite indispensable; and though the theatre might be put to it at first to find men and women of the necessary weight and experience at prices it could afford to pay, a little bold experiment and the further experience of good work done in the theatre should create within a year or two a solid body of this degree of talent. But once created it must be kept intact. In it would lie the theatre's resistant strength. Repertory work, which throws much responsibility upon the individual actor, simply cannot be done unless the middle ranks of the company are to be relied on. These actors would have to be well paid, and, in a moderate degree, increasingly well paid. To them more than to others doubtless—for they would not tend to be very young—the pension fund

* Upon the question of training, and the use of students in the theatre, see chapter xv.

would be an attraction. But the theatre could not afford first to make or increase their reputations by giving them chances which other theatres denied them, and then, as a result, to lose them. There is the salary at which one can obtain an actor; but one must think besides of the salary at which he can be kept. It is these middle ranks, then, that account for the forty-eight salaries which climb from £500 a year to £1,000. They would cost the theatre £27,800 a year; but they would be worth it, and it would be the poorest economy to try and cheapen them.

The third thing, however, which became clear was that it would be quite impossible for the theatre to pay its leading actors at anything like market rates. Thanks partly to America (to the ease and frequency with which actors and plays of reputation travel back and forth across the Atlantic), and partly to the cinema's competition, these have risen enormously within the last few years; and now the Talkie bids fair, for the moment, to send them even higher. It is a gambling market, truly, but it is a genuine one. Salaries of £250, £200, and £150 a week in New York, guaranteed for from ten to twenty weeks, are reflected as £150, £100, and £80 in London; and for cinema-work these may in either case be doubled, sometimes more than doubled. Nor is it only actors of world-shaking reputation who command them; but just good leading actors, whose reputation happens to be for some reason in the ascendant, or whose personality has a certain scarcity value. They cannot, of course, earn these sums for fifty-two weeks in the year. Five or ten years hence they may not be earning them so easily, if at all, while other actors may—who is to tell? But they are genuinely earning them now. The

64

National Theatre needs actors of this calibre; it needs better. Clearly it cannot compete in such a market. And to say that it must create leading actors of its own is no answer. Then the same market will be open to *them*, and no contracts will bind them. This is the tale told in every State theatre in Europe to-day.

The right thing would seem to be to establish a moral maximum, beyond which the theatre would, in no instance, go. This is set, it will be seen, at £2,500 a year. It is not meant to bear any relation to the £5,000 or £10,000 a year that an actor in the full tide of his success might, for a few years, gather in. It stands, in permanence, for a good solid income upon which, even in these days, a man may live very well; it bears (as do the £2,000, £1,750, and £1,500 which are its runners-up) a right relation to the middle range of salaries; it is, finally, all that a National Theatre ought to pay. And if an actor does not want to do the supremely interesting work which the Theatre would offer him in better, humaner conditions than can be found elsewhere, if he does not positively prefer this to the work that will gain him those precarious thousands more— well, once again, he is not the sort of actor the theatre wants; that is the last word on the matter.

But there are men and women who will positively prefer what the National Theatre has to offer them; one need not doubt it. The best men, and above all the best artists, are not moved by lust of money-making. Still, money counts; and it will be wiser not to expect them to take too altruistic an attitude; more especially because, with definite advantage to the theatre besides, they can be given an occasional chance of making the best of both worlds.

65   F

Furloughs

It is suggested that, after an actor has served six consecutive years in the theatre, the Director shall have power to give him, not oftener than once every three or four years, a year's furlough, with suspension of salary, of course, but without loss of seniority or interest in the pension fund. This will enable him to exploit elsewhere—probably very profitably—the reputation which the theatre and his work in it will have gained him. The holiday from its routine may be artistically refreshing for him too. Yet at the furlough's end he may be glad to come back to the theatre's solider work; yet again, he may bring new ideas with him when he comes. From the theatre's point of view, his temporary absence will shake up the settled order of things a little, which may always be in danger—as far, at any rate, as the 'classic' repertory is concerned—of becoming too settled; it will give other deserving actors a chance at his parts; and it will—here also is a danger—prevent habitual audiences from becoming perhaps a trifle bored by his too-constant appearances. They will welcome him the more heartily when they see him again.

Note that the furlough is to be for a complete year, and that it will be for the Director to grant it if and when he thinks fit. There is to be nothing like the *congés* at the Comédie Française, which let actors run off at all sorts of odd times and utterly disorganise the working of the theatre.*

* The director may fairly constantly have to choose between granting a furlough whether he wishes to or no and losing an actor. One year's absence in every three, however, should be the maximum permitted. The furloughs are, of course, not accounted for in the present numbering and pricing of the company, for they would be furloughs without pay. What is set out here is the company's working strength for any year. From five

66

Certain of the actors (not necessarily the leading ones, however) might be enabled to supplement their guaranteed income and vary their work by the production of plays—plays in which they did not appear. There are actors who become good producers without ceasing to be good actors, and the theatre would profit by variety in methods of production.

The Producers

In the main, however, this work, which is very specialised, would fall to the three producers. They are ranked in the company, but they would not exactly be of it; in closer relation, actually, to the Director and the general staff. They might do, at most, five or six productions a year each, big and small. But that would not be all their work, for they would be responsible for the artistic upkeep of any play they had produced, and this asks constant supervision and the rehearsing of new-comers to the cast, re-rehearsing of the old cast very often. It is more for this that each would receive his £1,000 a year. For each new production a certain fee would be added; how large a one could most fairly be made to depend upon the importance of the work involved. Their total incomes would probably reach £2,000 a year; an exceptional man doing exceptional work might command £2,500. It is perhaps a question whether their engagements should be permanent. They must know the company well, the strength and weakness of each individual in it; with the Director they would be largely responsible for casting the plays. But there would have to be

---

to ten actors might be on furlough at one time; the theatre's work probably could not afford more disturbance than this would imply.

some safeguard against staleness, a greater danger to producers than to actors even. Extended furloughs might be enough to secure this.

Extras

The 'walking on,' and as far as possible the 'supering' (there is a subtle distinction between the two humilities), might, it is to be hoped, be done by students from the two or three good schools of acting that now exist.* But even students must not work for nothing, must not, at any rate, be out of pocket by working. Two thousand pounds a year is set down for their expenses. It would be none too much.

* See chapter xv. for the further discussion of this.

CHAPTER VII

THE REPERTORY AND ITS COST

Yearly expenditure   £33,250

The Repertory Itself

Here, *for the sake of illustration merely*, are forty-nine plays which might make up the repertory for any year, once the theatre were well established.*

<table>
<tr><td>LARGE HOUSE</td><td>SMALL HOUSE</td></tr>
</table>

New Plays

LARGE HOUSE	SMALL HOUSE
Saint Cecilia	*The Trumpet of Peace*
The Flight of the Duchess	*These Bright Young*
The Chiltern Hundreds	*Things*
The Magnet	*Peradventure*
	The Man who would be
	King
	The Long Road
	Here we are again

The titles are, of course, invented for this occasion, or borrowed. They stand for new plays, but not necessarily new productions; four of them at least may be accounted successes of last year carried on. Among the authors should be some of the younger dramatists who are not represented in the list of modern revivals below.

* This number of one less than fifty has been somewhat fortuitously arrived at only by the inclusion of the History cycle. If we think of that as four plays in one, the number becomes one more than forty-five. The repertory would normally run to between forty-five and fifty plays a year, probably.

LARGE HOUSE	SMALL HOUSE

Shakespeare

Hamlet	*The Comedy of Errors*
Antony and Cleopatra	*The Tempest*
Othello	
Richard II	
Henry IV, part 1	
Henry IV, part 2	
Henry V	
Romeo and Juliet	
Twelfth Night	
A Midsummer Night's Dream	

Twelve plays out of forty-nine may seem too high a proportion even for Shakespeare. But the historical series, which would usually be played as a series (not necessarily on four consecutive performances), may in a sense be counted as one. It is set down to show the sort of thing a National Theatre should and would do, which practically no other theatre (Stratford, perhaps, apart) will or can do. The theatre should, moreover, be under an obligation to have at least one play of Shakespeare's in the bill each week, and to give not less than one hundred and fifty performances of his plays in the year. But a number of these might be performances specially organised for students and schools; and this is one of the reasons why these plays are set down predominantly for the large house. But if they were played in a more or less conventionalised setting (and, personally, I should hope they would be), they, and other plays so treated, could very simply be transferred from one house to the other.

LARGE HOUSE	SMALL HOUSE

Classic, Mediæval, Minor Elizabethan

The Agamemnon	*The Faithful Shepherdess*
Everyman	*The Feast of Bacchus*
	(arranged from Terence
	by Robert Bridges)

These imply student and school performances too.

Eighteenth-century Comedy

The School for Scandal	*Love for Love*

Revivals of modern English plays

(or, to avoid controversy, call them plays written in the English language)

The Admirable Crichton	*Preserving Mr. Panmure*
John Bull's Other Island	*An Irish Triple Bill*
Strife	(Yeats, Synge, Lady
Hassan	Gregory)
The Importance of Being Earnest	*The Faithful Jane Clegg*
The Mollusc	*The Constant Wife*
The Return of the Prodigal	*The Great Adventure*

One is immediately struck by the omissions from this list. There could be no better proof of the wide field of choice for plays which could probably command good audiences for from ten to thirty performances in any year (granted good performances of them), plays which, if this is all they can command, are at present left in oblivion.

71

LARGE HOUSE	SMALL HOUSE

Translations

LARGE HOUSE	SMALL HOUSE
Le Bourgeois Gentil-homme	*The Thieves' Comedy (der Biberpelz)*
Peer Gynt	*Pelleas and Melisande*
The Kingdom of God	*The Three Sisters*
The Wild Duck	*There are Crimes and Crimes*

Here, besides the recognised classics, we have, as in the list of English revivals, some plays of admittedly minority appeal, and some which need such quality of performance as only a theatre devoting as much care to the play that will not earn large profits as to the play that will can give.

There need be no lack of material for the repertory, that is evident. Any play that was good of its kind would have a claim to be admitted and any kind of play that the theatre could cast and stage.

For the benefit of those who do not easily visualise the working of a repertory here are two specimen fortnights. The first falls in the winter holiday season. The large house is given up mainly to Shakespeare, and is playing no less than four matinées a week. This is, of course, exceptional. But even the small house is giving three. The bracketed figures show roughly the number of actors and actresses employed in each performance.

LARGE HOUSE	SMALL HOUSE

Wednesday, January 1

LARGE HOUSE	SMALL HOUSE
Twelfth Night matinée (14 m., 3 w.)	*The Importance of Being Earnest* matinée (5 m., 4 w.)
Antony and Cleopatra (34 m., 4 w.)	*The Long Road*

LARGE HOUSE	SMALL HOUSE

Thursday, January 2

A Midsummer Night's Dream matinée (13 m., 4 w.)
Peer Gynt (30 m., 22 w.)

The Great Adventure (15 m., 3 w.)

Friday, January 3

Antony and Cleopatra (34 m., 4 w.)

The Long Road matinée
The Thieves' Comedy (9 m., 4 w.)

Saturday, January 4

Antony and Cleopatra matinée (34 m., 4 w.)
A Midsummer Night's Dream (13 m., 4 w.)

Irish Triple Bill matinée (12 m., 8 w.)
The Long Road

Monday, January 6

Twelfth Night (14 m., 3 w.)

The Importance of Being Earnest (5 m., 4 w.)

Tuesday, January 7

The Magnet matinée
Antony and Cleopatra (34 m., 4 w.)

The Long Road

Wednesday, January 8

A Midsummer Night's Dream matinée (13 m., 4 w.)
The School for Scandal (12 m., 4 w.)

The Great Adventure matinée (15 m., 3 w.)
Irish Triple Bill (12 m., 8 w.)

Thursday, January 9

Antony and Cleopatra matinée (34 m., 4 w.)
The Magnet

The Importance of Being Earnest (5 m., 4 w.)

73

LARGE HOUSE	SMALL HOUSE

Friday, January 10

	The Comedy of Errors
The Admirable Crichton	matinée (14 m., 5 w.)
(13 m., 10 w.)	*The Long Road*

Saturday, January 11

The Magnet matinée	*The Long Road* matinée
Antony and Cleopatra	*The Thieves' Comedy* (9
(34 m., 4 w.)	m., 4 w.)

Monday, January 13

The School for Scandal	*The Long Road*
(12 m., 4 w.)	

Tuesday, January 14

The Admirable Crichton	
matinée (13 m., 10 w.)	*The Great Adventure* (15
Hamlet (22 m., 2 w.)	m., 3 w.)

Antony and Cleopatra we may suppose a recent and successful revival. It is given six performances in the fortnight. For the rest, Shakespearean comedy is in the ascendant, *A Midsummer Night's Dream* being particularly a holiday play. But *Twelfth Night* would never be long absent from the repertory, nor *Hamlet*. *The Magnet*, a new play, occupies the large house for three performances; it may be a successful production now some six months old. *The Long Road* has seven performances in the small house; this stands for a new play more recently produced and very fairly successful. *The School for Scandal* would never be long absent from the bill. The modern revivals speak for themselves.

The numerical capacity of the company is never very hardly strained. On the evening of January 2 forty-five men and twenty-five women are acting in the two houses together, forty-six men and twelve women on the evening of Saturday, January 4.*

For a second specimen fortnight:

LARGE HOUSE	SMALL HOUSE

Wednesday, October 1

	These Bright Young Things matinée
The Chiltern Hundreds	*Love for Love* (10 m., 6 w.)

Thursday, October 2

The Chiltern Hundreds matinée	*These Bright Young Things*
Othello (18 m., 3 w.)	

Friday, October 3

The Chiltern Hundreds	*The Long Road*

Saturday, October 4

Agamemnon matinée (21 m., 2 w.)	*Love for Love* matinée (10 m., 6 w.)
The Chiltern Hundreds	*The Tempest* (16 m., 7 w.)

* But let anyone who may object that a smaller company than that here planned for could do the work remember that—besides the discount which must be made for absence, illness, understudying, and for the fact that parts must not be cast unsuitably—it would be extravagant to pay actors who command large fees to play parts which should only command small ones. For artistic and financial reasons too, as well as from consideration of the strain on them of overwork, it can never be economical to have the entire company absorbed in the casts night after night.

LARGE HOUSE   SMALL HOUSE

Monday, October 6

Romeo and Juliet (21 m.,   *The Wild Duck*
4 w.)

Tuesday, October 7

The Chiltern Hundreds   *These Bright Young
                            Things*

Wednesday, October 8

                            The Feast of Bacchus
                            matinée
John Bull's Other Island   *The Wild Duck* (20 m.,
(10 m., 2 w.)   3 w.)

Thursday, October 9

Richard II matinée (36
m., 4 w.)   *Love for Love* (10 m., 6
The Chiltern Hundreds   w.)

Friday, October 10

The Chiltern Hundreds   *Peradventure*

Saturday, October 11

Henry IV, Pt. 1 matinée   *The Return of the Prodi-
(35 m., 3 w.)   gal* matinée (10 m., 5
                            w.)
Henry IV, Pt. 2 (44 m.,   *These Bright Young
4 w.)   Things*

76

LARGE HOUSE   SMALL HOUSE

Monday, October 13

The Chiltern Hundreds   *The Long Road*

Tuesday, October 14

Henry V (45 m., 4 w.)   *Love for Love* (10m., 6w.)

The Chiltern Hundreds is a new play and is a success. It is drawing full houses, and is being acted, for the moment, as often as is compatible with the interests of the rest of the repertory. It is given eight performances in the fortnight. There is no reason that more matinées should not be added. In the small house another new play, *These Bright Young Things*, is fairly successful, and is given four performances in the fortnight: yet another, *Peradventure*, is (as befits its title) a more doubtful affair, and it has only one. *The Long Road*, which was being played in January, is still alive: we may suppose that there is a steady three parts of a houseful for it once a week. *Love for Love* looks like a recent revival; if it is really well done it will gather audiences, though not in crowds, about twice a week for a month or so. Good acting granted, an occasional revival of *The Wild Duck* will not lack support, nor will a performance or so of St. John Hankin's admirably bitter-sweet comedy; nor a few, even more than a few, of Bernard Shaw's masterpiece. *The Feast of Bacchus* is an experiment. *Agamemnon* and the Shakespeares stand for the steady ' classic ' repertory—kept from becoming too steady by occasional changes of cast. The inclusion of the History cycle should be noted, with the complete *Henry IV* given on the Saturday. Devotees may find a meal in the theatre's restaurant between the performances.

77

The Cost

What would the staging of these forty-nine plays cost? We must make certain assumptions. First, that all the scenery, properties, and costumes (except for such modern dresses, uniforms, and furniture as it would obviously be better to buy or contract for elsewhere) would be made and painted in the theatre.

This is indisputably the best plan. And here what we have called the ' economic dimension ' of the theatre comes in very definitely. It will not pay a theatre doing only three or four productions a year to keep its own workshops going, any more than it would pay a publisher producing a dozen books to keep his own press and bindery. The idle intervals will wipe out all saving—and more. But if you can (as in this case you could) keep your workmen constantly employed, that is quite another matter: twenty to twenty-five per cent can be saved upon contract prices, especially if nothing has to be written down for the rent of your workshops.

The second assumption is that the productions in current use would be stored under the theatre roof. You cannot cart scenery, or even furniture, about without rapidly ruining it.

The third assumption is that scenery would be as far as possible standardised, so that there would be a large percentage of salvage in the productions of plays that were failures. New designing and re-painting there would constantly be; but well-built and carefully handled scenery will last.

For a fourth assumption, there would be none of the vast extravagances of paint and carpentry by which a past generation of producers tried to make Shakespeare popular. Even if a conventional stage were not the rule, the play and not the scenery would be the thing. Costuming might, and should be, costly. But good costumes have much wear in them; they are, moreover, as to a great part of Shakespeare (and to an even greater for eighteenth-century comedy), discreetly interchangeable between play and play.

Into the cost of a production is here counted material, workmanship, designing, the producer's fee, the composer's (if there should be incidental music), the cost of dress rehearsals (but not of others).

The wages of carpenters, property-makers, and wardrobe-workers have not been separately estimated; it being simpler—and not misleading—to state the production costs as a whole. In practice the method might be different, for the superintendence of the work would be in the hands of the chief stage manager and the head carpenter (whose full salaries are set down elsewhere) and there would be much interchange of labour between workshop and stage. Wardrobe workers would often act as dressers, and their pay in that capacity is set down elsewhere. Producers' fees might vary between £100 and £200, might on occasion exceed this; they are, it will be remembered, a supplement to salaries.

Designers' fees could vary from £50 for designs for a scene or two to £400-£500 for the complete designing—scenes, costumes, properties and all— of such a production as, say, *Hassan*. It would be a mistake to attach one designer permanently to the theatre; as much variety as possible would be wanted here. But when the issues are quite simple, most producers know—or should know—what they want, and both the scenic artist and the head of the

79

wardrobe would be capable of carrying it out unaided.

As to dress rehearsals, a heavy item for a big production in an ordinary theatre, they should not be
so very costly. Actors accustomed to the stages and
the houses would not need so many; and the
standardisation of the scenery and the constant
working of the stage machinery by a staff that was
as accustomed to it should do much to eliminate
overtime.

Taking all these things into account, then, one
may be justified in setting down the average gross
cost of production at—

£2,500 in the large house,
£1,500 in the small house,

the difference between the two lying less in the
size of the stages than in the fact that the plays with
small casts and simpler staging are, as a rule, to be
found in the small house.

It is a rough-and-ready estimate, certainly. For
the large house one is striking an average between
productions of *Hassan*, *Peer Gynt*, and an elaborately
costumed *Antony and Cleopatra*, which might each
cost from £5,000 to £6,000, and such plays as *John
Bull's Other Island* and *Strife*, which could certainly, under these conditions, be put on for £1,000
each, probably less. Once the practicabilities of a
Greek stage are provided, the material for a production of *Agamemnon* is in the costumes, which
are neither very numerous nor very costly. Over
some of the Shakespeare, at any rate, there will
certainly be a saving in conventionalised scenery
and a partial duplication of costume. And this we
may exemplify here and now by calculating the
four Histories as three productions only.

In the small house the average has to be struck between *Pelleas and Melisande* and *The Faithful*, which might well cost £2,000 and £2,500 apiece, and *Jane Clegg* and *The Thieves' Comedy*, which could be done for £200 and £250 each without much difficulty.

Then the life of a production must be considered. It need not, of course—unless the play to which it belonged were permanently in the repertory or such a success that it was worn out in this one service— be considered as solely and integrally connected with a particular play. As we have said, when its immediate use was past the salvage in material and even in workmanship would be considerable. Scenery is repaintable, in some cases it can be put to other use as it is. Costumes have a varying lease of life, and armour is all but immortal. Furniture, well cared for, lasts long, and once a large stock of it has accumulated, expenditure here should be comparatively small. Taking all this into account, and striking our average of cost between the scene-painting that might only serve for a dozen per-formances, the particular dresses with a salvage value of no more than ten per cent, and the scene material which could be used for ten more plays, the costumes for twenty with a little cost for altera-tion, the furniture which would serve for another hundred, we may fairly put the 'life' of a pro-duction at four years.

Twenty-three productions, then, in the large house, at an average of £2,500 each, show a capital cost of £57,500.* Twenty-five productions in the small house, at an average of £1,500, show a capital cost of £37,500. We divide this sum by four (years) to show the net capital cost of a year's

* The four Histories (see p. 80) counting as three.

productions. But there is also upkeep to be considered; repairs, cleaning of costumes, their occasional alteration and renewal. We must put this down at ten per cent. This gives us—

Large House: twenty-three productions at an average of £2,500	£57,500
Small House: twenty-five productions at an average of £1,500	37,500
	£95,000
This divided by four (years)	£23,750
Ten per cent of £95,000 for upkeep	9,500
	£33,250

In practice, of course, the working out of the business would be far more complex. The theatre might stage twenty or more apparently new productions a year (new plays and revivals included) with not more than four or five of these brand new throughout in material and workmanship. The rest would be new in varying percentages from seventy-five to twenty-five per cent; and with taste and careful contriving, audiences would be little the wiser. For productions in the permanent repertory, and for those carried over intact from the year before, even from the year before that, the ten per cent for upkeep should suffice.

CHAPTER VIII

AUTHORS' ROYALTIES AND THE PENSION FUND

Ten per cent deducted from estimated
gross receipts   £20,460

I T is proposed to deduct ten per cent from the
gross receipts of every performance: for the author
if the play is copyright; if it is non-copyright, for
the pension fund.

This hard-and-fast and symmetrical plan has
several advantages. It would, as we have seen, feed
the pension fund satisfactorily and avoid actual
deductions from salaries for the purpose. It would
free the management from all temptation to prefer,
for economy's sake, non-copyright to copyright
plays. This is important. The theatre must not
neglect modern authors, nor must Shakespeare
hold his place there as a blackleg.

Copyright plays would possibly account for
nearly three-fifths of the repertory, and a larger
percentage of performances, though this would not
necessarily mean a proportionate share of the receipts; for more often than not they would find
their way into the smaller house. In all, authors'
royalties might amount in a year to between
£12,000 and £14,000.

By bargaining over each play this could probably
be a little reduced. But it would be a penny-wise
and pound-foolish policy. Some foreign plays, old
plays, plays by untried authors could doubtless be

had more cheaply. But if a fixed ten per cent is generous here, bargaining with an author whose plays had a reputation for long runs for a production of one of them in repertory might well lead to opposite results. The hard-and-fast rule would be something of a safeguard. So would another, by which the theatre would renounce all further exploiting of a play once its own use for it was satisfied—and of the author. This may seem wanton neglect of opportunity. Most managers see themselves occasionally making the fortune of some neglected dramatist by having the wit to produce a many times rejected play—and then legitimately sharing both the first fruits and a second harvest.

But, in the first place, the National Theatre will be to some extent a public institution, and public institutions must not—upon whatever excuse—profiteer. In the second, as we said, if the author who comes suing must pay the price, when the theatre sues it will have to pay in turn, and the gain on the balance will be doubtful. As with the leading actors, there can be no competing in the open market. The popular author of a popular play will always be able to make more out of a long run, even though a hundred performances in the year in the large house here (and this would mean exceptional success) might bring him £4,000. With bargaining admissible there would soon be demands for twelve or fifteen per cent as compensation for his sacrifice, and the privilege of withdrawing the play after fifty performances if he found he could do better with it elsewhere. No, the theatre will be in a far safer, as well as a far more dignified, position if it can say " This is our rule, we think it a fair one and we never depart from it. We give you for your play what you cannot well get elsewhere, unscamped preparation and performance by a highly organised and individually efficient company. We do everything possible to make it a success, and all the contingent advantages are yours, you pay us no tax on them." Dramatists seldom or never complain—publicly at any rate—that they have been 'let down' by the actors of a play. They know—or should—under what difficulties and strain actors work, and how much undeserving plays may owe to them. But many a dramatist, with a difficult play in hand, would prefer such quality of performance as the National Theatre could offer to every seeming prospect of long-run and more popular success. And, after all, three or four thousand pounds and a free market elsewhere is not such a poor material reward.*

For a last consideration, it is easily possible that the dramatists would get together, and either by public pressure upon the Trustees or—in emulation of the Société des Auteurs Dramatiques and the American Dramatists' Guild—through the Authors' Society insist upon equal treatment for all.

---

* One qualification may be made. Should the National Theatre have touring companies connected with it (see chapter xv.), it could legitimately ask rights in the plays for them. And this might be a proper matter for bargaining.

CHAPTER IX

THE STAFF

Salaries in front	£18,966
Stage salaries	20,831
	£39,797

T H E above is the customary division. Here follow salaries for the front of the theatre in detail, with comments upon each numbered item of them.

		£
(1)	The Director's Secretary	700
	The Director's Typist	250
	The Business Manager's Secretary-typist	250
(2)	Acting Manager; large house	900
	Acting Manager; small house	750
	Press Representative	750
	Typist	250
(3)	Box Office Manager	700
	First Assistant	500
	Second Assistant	400
	Third and Fourth Assistant at £350 each	700
	Typist	250
	Two Telephone Boys at £75 each	150
(4)	Six Money-takers at 4s. a perf. (880 perf.)	1,056
	Twelve Check-takers at 3s. a perf. (880 perf.)	1,584
(5)	Twenty-five Cleaners at £2 a week each	2,600
(6)	Twenty Ushers (large house) at £2 a week each	2,080
	Fifteen Ushers (small house) at £2 a week each	1,560
	Fifteen Cloak-room Attendants (large house) at £2 a week each	1,560
	Ten Cloak-room Attendants (small house) at £2 a week each	1,040
	Six Linkmen at £3 a week each	936
		£18,966

(1) A difficult and important job, for any director would need a tactful and effective buffer between him and the thousand and one people who would think they had a right to waste his time. This, to mention only one of his duties. It would be a young man's job, nevertheless.

(2) An 'acting manager,' it may have to be explained to the layman, is responsible for, among other matters, the front of the house during a performance; and this is always an important, on occasion may be a serious responsibility. The senior of the two would replace the business manager when necessary, and, strictly speaking, some relief should be provided for them also; but this could possibly be found among the staff as it stands.

(3) There should, of course, be only one box office for the two houses, as far as organisation goes. This would unify the public's interest in their work and make the transference of bookings from one to the other easy. But it would be a busy and—with a repertory to deal with—it would have to be a very efficient box office. All seats in the theatre would be bookable.

(4) In view of the fact that all the seats could be booked, only six money-takers are provided. The number of check-takers depends on the theatre's planning; twelve might well not be enough, but, with good planning, it should be. The work is part-time work, usually done by men who have employment elsewhere. It would certainly be better, and it might be possible, to abolish part-time work (at any rate some of it) by providing other employment about the theatre. But this cannot properly be calculated on.

(5) The cleaning of this theatre, with its rehearsal rooms and offices in constant use, and its never-ending use of the stage for performance or rehearsal, would be a problem best to be solved

by a smaller better-paid staff and a full instalment of machinery. But one can only budget at the moment for this unsatisfactory and quite costly, though ill-paid (once again part-time), handiwork.

(6) These salaries could, at a pinch, be eliminated or at least provided for apart, by the sale of programmes and a charge for the care of hats and coats. The subject is discussed in chapter xiii., as it is connected with the question of the refreshment rooms and their profits.

Stage salaries in detail:

		£
(1)	Chief Stage Manager	1,500
	His Typist-secretary	250
(2)	Stage Manager; large house	900
	Stage Manager; small house	750
(3)	Librarian	500
	Two Call-boys at 36s. a week each (say)	190
	Head Fireman at £4 16s. a week (say)	250
	Three Assistant Firemen at £2 16s. a week each (say)	437
(4)	Housekeeper (with rooms in theatre)	500
	Assistant	200
(5)	Stage-door Keeper (with rooms in theatre)	250
	Assistant	200
	Second Assistant	150
(6)	Chief Master-carpenter	600
	Master-carpenter; large house	400
	Master-carpenter; small house	350
	Twelve Day Men at (say) £5 a week each	3,120
	Twelve Night Men at (say) £1 16s. a week each	1,123
(7)	Property-master	400
	Six Day Men at (say) £5 a week each	1,560
	Twelve Night Men at (say) £1 16s. a week each	1,123
(8)	Chief Electrician	500
	Head Assistant	350
	Three Day Men at (say) £5 a week each	780
	Two Cleaners at (say) £2 a week each	208
	Twelve Night Men at £1 16s. a week each	1,120
(9)	Thirty Dressers at £2 a week each	3,120

£20,831

These figures require general as well as, in some cases, particular explanation. They are not all calculated upon the same basis. Certain of the salaries may seem over-generous. For instance, a chief stage manager could be found for much less than £1,500 a year, and a master carpenter for less than £600. But the work asked of these heads of departments is very responsible, and they would save the theatre the amount of their salaries many times over by organising it well. Now the organising brain commands good pay. Moreover, to repeat what has been many times said, these figures refer to a year's operation when the theatre shall have been, perhaps, ten years in existence. These posts might not be so highly salaried to begin with, but it would be above all things important to keep the holders of them—if they were worth keeping— permanently in the theatre's service. Only so, in- deed, could the complex stage arrangements be smoothly put through. And continued good ser- vice must be recognised by increase of pay. On the other hand are their prospects of good pen- sions.

The 'day men' and 'night men' are put down at present trade-union rates. The pay is apt to be considerably increased by scene rehearsals (the cost of which is hidden in production expenses), but then it is calculated upon a basis at once costly to the theatre and as demoralising to the men as any- thing like casual labour is bound to be. Clearly it would be better to organise the work—as it well could be organised—upon a system of constant em- ployment. But, at present, one can only set out esti- mates on these terms.

(1) He would be responsible for the organisation of the workshops, of the two stages with their con-

tinual variation of rehearsal and performance, for the allotment of rehearsal rooms, and for all staff discipline behind the scenes.

(2) In charge of the actual working of their stages (even the layman nowadays does not need telling that they would have nothing to do with the rehearsing of the actors). The senior of them would replace the chief stage manager during his absences.

(3) He would be responsible for the keeping of prompt books, parts, designs, and models. He would act as relief to the two stage managers. Under General Expenses a sum will be found allotted to the typing of plays and parts—a considerable business in a repertory. If it proved cheaper to do this in the theatre, the small staff would work under the librarian. It is not suggested that he should be in charge of the library (properly so called) in front of the house. That would be another sort of business.

N.B. It will be noticed that no provision is made for assistant stage managers, that is to say prompters, whose duty it is to follow the rehearsals, and at performances to follow the action, see the actors are ready, give the curtain and light signals, etc. This work would be better done by young actors (probably those in their probationary year), of whom two should be attached to each production. It would be, for one thing, in moderation, an admirable training for them, the quickest way to bring them into the swim of the theatre. They would, of course, be given simple productions to deal with at first; and the stage manager, upon whom responsibility devolves the moment the play passes from the rehearsal room to the stage, could be trusted to help them.

(4) A post differing greatly in degree from that

of the ordinary theatre housekeeper, and almost in kind; for this theatre would be constantly occupied by day, and the wardrobes, offices, dressing and rehearsal rooms, quite apart from the public side of the theatre, would give ample employment both to a first-rate housekeeper and an assistant.

(5) The entrance—a multiple entrance, probably, common to workshops, rehearsal rooms and to both stages—would have to be carefully constructed, so that, in the interests of discipline and time-keeping, the comings and goings of actors and staff could be accurately noted. Three men would be none too many for this sixteen hours of duty.

(6) The chief stage manager's lieutenant in the scenic workshops. But, as he must also have control of the stages and scene-stores, his salary properly appears here instead of being hidden in production expenses.

(7) The old-style property-master made many more of his properties than does his descendant to-day. The theatre might restore the old system, in which case a head of this department analogous to the chief master carpenter would be needed. The wages-cost would in that case be extracted from the present production expenses.

(8) This, again, envisages things as they are. The salary stands for a small increase on trades-union rates. But it is possible that a comprehensive electrical equipment—*not* for scenic 'stunts,' but for the easier manœuvring of the multiplied material of the repertory—might make this post a more important one, commanding higher pay. There should then be saving elsewhere.

(9) This is generally accounted part-time work, and these rates of pay are a slight increase upon the usual ones (but the customary tips probably raise

them by another 15s.—£1 a week). This is the average number of dressers that might be required. A proportion of them would also be employed in the wardrobe, and their pay for this work is (again) hidden in production expenses.

CHAPTER X
MUSIC

Conductor	£1,200
Leader	700
Twenty musicians	7,500
	£9,400

S O M E permanent provision for music there must be. It is not a question of taste. A large proportion of plays in the repertory will demand incidental music, and of varying sorts. It would be difficult, and very extravagant, to engage this specially.

Nor would the suppression of inter-act music probably be a wise policy. English audiences are used to it; and, if it is at all worth listening to, it adds—sometimes quite disproportionately—to the pleasure of the occasion. But a theatre that had, as this would have, a foyer in which, between the acts, its audience could walk or sit about, could far better establish its orchestra there than in the house itself where the orchestra pit is an awkward survival. The advantages are obvious. The house is aired, the audience is refreshed. And, with two houses having a common foyer, the plan would work even better, for one orchestra will serve for the two. Act intervals would sometimes, but not often, coincide. The orchestra would be playing for some five or six ten-minute spaces in an evening.

Incidental music seldom requires a full orchestra; the sections of it that were needed for this could be, for the time, detached. In Shakespearean productions, for instance, it is largely trumpets, horns and drums that are required.

But if there is to be music at all, it must be good of its kind, and done with some completeness. The Mustel-organ and the too valiantly thumped piano are not admissible in the full light and exposure of a foyer.

The conductor's salary supposes a musician of some authority and accomplishment, who would also select—occasionally compose—the incidental music for the plays.* The leader would conduct this incidental music, or take the conductor's place when he himself wished to. The pay for the twenty musicians is set down at generously interpreted trades-union rates.

* Fees for its composition (hidden in production expenses) would add something to his salary.

CHAPTER XI

GENERAL EXPENSES

(1)	Advertising	£9,000
(2)	Printing	1,500
	Stationery, telephone, postage, petty cash, and sundries	3,000
	Lighting and heating	5,000
(3)	Insurance	1,000
	Accountancy	1,000
(4)	Typing and binding of scripts, etc.	700
(5)	Library	600
		£21,800

THE chief thing to note about these figures is (paradoxically) the omissions from them. No provision is made for rates and taxes, nor for the upkeep of the building, nor for the depreciation of its equipment and furniture, nor would this insurance cover much more than employer's liability and movables. The running of the theatre should perhaps be debited with all these things. My reason for leaving them out of account here is, frankly, that their presence or absence makes just the difference between the need for a current subsidy and none. The money must be found, of course; and if the theatre cannot earn it, a subsidy must supply it. But this still would not mean the subsidising of the actual dramatic work done. Part of the money might well be earned if the theatre prospered; say, the depreciation fund and full insurance premiums. But rates and taxes alone—even apart from the

95

present outrageous entertainment tax—could well amount to between £5,000 and £10,000 a year.* Now if a subsidy were needed to cover this, *but no more than this*, it would only be fair to the theatre and its work that the fact should be made plain. For the Government or the Municipality would merely be returning with one hand what they had taken away with the other.

Here are comments on the individual items as they now stand.

(1) This allows £7,000 a year for bare announcement of the repertory in the chief newspapers (this should be regularly done, and never more), and £2,000 a year for the weekly posting and ' inspection ' of bills large enough to set out the current fortnight's repertory at, say, five hundred railway and omnibus stations.

(2) This is for the printing of posters and programmes. If (unhappily) it were decided to sell the programmes there would be an actual saving here and—see chapter xiii.—a contingent credit created.

(3) This, as we have noted, is meant to cover personal effects and employer's liability. It would possibly suffice for scenery and stage furniture too.

(4) This, for contract work, is a low estimate. Some economy might be effected by organising all the typing of whatever sort in one department.

(5) As the library is shown on the building plan, it is right to make modest provision for its running. This would also provide for the keeping of the theatre bookstall, in which there is a small profit and much legitimately excellent advertisement.

---

* Since writing this, however, the Royal Academy of Dramatic Art has (at last) been relieved of the obligation to pay rates on the ground, long disputed, that acting *is* a 'fine art'. The National Theatre, then, could presumably claim exemption too.

CHAPTER XII

POSSIBLE RECEIPTS

T H E large house is to hold, let us say, 1,850 people. From this we subtract fifty seats to account for the average number of complimentary admissions. Ordinarily there should not be so many (the theatre would never be ' papered '), but at first performances there would be more, unless the newspapers all adopted the one-time admirable practice of *The Times* and paid for their critics' stalls.

Large House : capacity 1,800

				£	s.	d.
275	seats at	10s. 6d.		£144	7	
275	,, ,,	7s. 6d.		103	3	
475	,, ,,	5s. 0d.		118	15	
475	,, ,,	2s. 6d.		59	7	
300	,, ,,	1s. 0d.		15	0	
1,800				£440	12	

The average takings should be two-thirds of this capacity: say, £293.

There are to be 440 performances a year: an average of eight a week with extra matinées to be given mainly in holiday time (twenty-six extra matinées must be given to make up the 440 performances, as on Christmas Day and Good Friday there are none at all).

440 performances at £293 £128,920

H

The small house is to hold 1,050. For the same reasons we calculate its working capacity at 1,000.

Small House: capacity 1,000

175 seats at	10s. 6d.	£91	17
175 ,, ,,	7s. 6d.	65	13
250 ,, ,,	5s. 0d.	62	10
250 ,, ,,	2s. 6d.	31	5
150 ,, ,,	1s. 0d.	7	10
1,000		£258	15

Two-thirds of this capacity: say, £172.

440 performances at £172   £75,680

Large House	£128,920
Small House	75,680
	£204,600

The Prices of the Seats

These are the prices which normally obtained in West-end theatres before the war, and most managers are now doing all that the entertainment tax permits to restore them. The 1s. for the gallery is not an economic price. It is kept—where it is in effect kept—partly for sentiment, partly to meet the cinema competition, partly because in old-fashioned theatres the seats are so bad that it is a wonder anyone will sit in them. There must be no bad seats in a newly built National Theatre. If 1s. places are retained it will be out of sentiment, and so that no one who can raise that comparatively modest sum shall be able to say he is excluded. For many people, of course, it is still not a modest sum. They can be catered for with special and specially priced performances; but unless these are as specially—and quite frankly—subsidised the whole budget will be demoralised. This theatre is not planned as a cheap theatre, and to make it so in one sense must be almost certainly to make it so (and quite certainly to imply that it was so!) in another. Its scheme of prices should be that which ordinarily buys the best dramatic fare going. From another point of view, it should be kept free from the reproach of underselling private enterprise.

There is, however, no reason that the *incidence* of its prices should not be particularly favourable to the playgoer of moderate means; and it will be noticed that half the seats (in the large house rather more) are priced at 5s. and 2s. 6d. This is an important matter, and it is the architect, to begin with, who would have to give careful attention to it. Experience shows (there need be no invidious discussion of the reason) that, when any play of quality is produced in London, seats at about these prices are the first to fill and the last to empty.* A success crowds them out and the average theatre does not, of course, hold enough of them for their filling alone to pay. Nor indeed could it be made to in the National Theatre. But taking them altogether (the uneconomic 'shillings' included), the cheaper places could, by themselves, accumulate quite respectable receipts, and be a firm backbone to the theatre's income. But, further, the architect must provide for some elasticity; for the turning, on occasions, of a vacant row or so at 10s. 6d. and 7s. 6d. into extra rows at 7s. 6d. and 5s. and 2s. 6d. The theatre will sometimes need, by the reverse process, to exploit a success for a while, but it should never need to remove a play from its reper-

* See, for arguments for and against this statement, Appendix I, p. 121.

tory while any large number of playgoers of moderate means remain to patronise it.

Four Hundred and Forty Performances a Year in each House

This is not too many. Any popular cinema would think it far too few. The cinema industry soon made the fairly obvious discovery that the longer you can keep your shop open the lighter is the distributed burden of your overhead expenses. Thirty years ago the supposition still was that people would only go to entertainments in the evening and on the Saturday half-holiday. We have now learnt that, if an entertainment is good enough, there are—in a city the size of London at any rate—audiences to be found on any day of the week. The doctrine has, of course, its limitations; and a theatre has far more than the distribution of its overhead expenses to consider, it is burdened with a performance cost out of all proportion to the cinema's. And a theatre running one play only, offering the one entertainment at each and every performance, may pretty soon come to the end of the rather specialised audiences which will choose a Monday or Tuesday or Friday afternoon—if every other occasion is open to them too. There is also the strain on the actors to be considered. But a repertory theatre, with its variety of plays, and its duplication of actors, is not thus hampered. In theory, each house should be able to give twelve performances a week. In practice it could not—could not, at any rate, for more than a week or so together; the strain on the rest of the human mechanism would be too great. But there is no reason that it should not average eight throughout the year, and then add another twenty to thirty. There would be slack times, of course; performances on hot summer afternoons are not likely to be crowded. But the slack could be taken up, and mainly in two ways: by the prompt allotment of extra performances to a success (better policy than to let it thrust moderately profitable plays from the bill), and by the organising, more particularly at such times, of the special performances for students and schools, which it would be the theatre's duty to give.

These would have to be performances at reduced prices. They would need to be specially subsidised, it is true, but not so very heavily. If the large house were filled at 2s. 6d. and 1s. (and such organised performances should always be full) the takings would be £160; the small house at the same prices would hold £63. If the two-thirds normal capacity is to be taken as the 'economic price' of an average performance, we must have a subsidy of £133 for the large house and £109 for the small. Something over £7,000 a year, that is to say, would subsidise sixty cheap performances (thirty in each house), would give 85,000 students and school children a sight of a good play well acted. The Board of Education might do worse than sanction the expenditure.

An Average of Two-thirds Capacity

The experienced theatre manager may exclaim against the optimism of this. He has his successes, and can then rejoice in practically full houses for three or six months, or even for a year on end. But if he looks back over five years, his failures, bad weather, accidents of one sort or another, may have pulled the average of his takings very far down. Also, there has been commission (sometimes a heavy one) upon the sale of seats to be paid to the libraries.

But he must now think along different lines. Quite apart from its artistic advantages, the true repertory system stands as an economic indictment of the long-run system, and must so justify itself or fall. And with it must fall the whole scheme. If this ' average of two-thirds capacity ' cannot be made good, there can be no National Theatre. For who wants to see half-empty houses, heavily subsidised?

Compare the two systems from the economic point of view. With an overwhelming success the long-run manager is obviously satisfied. He is filling his theatre, he is spending money upon practically nothing but this one entertainment. Such a success is his highest aim, a most legitimate aim; and if he hits the mark of it once in every four tries he will do well. He has nothing else to consider; and the repertory theatre, which has—which, if it happens on such a success, cannot let it oust every other play from the bill, nor scrap every other expense—is for the moment at as obvious a disadvantage compared to him.

But such successes, needless to say, are not the common fare of the long-run theatres. They stand out as startling exceptions among moderately but still quite genuinely successful plays; though even to these must come the slack time when the public has had nearly but not quite enough of them, when the receipts fall to danger point and the manager must wait to see if they will rise again—and they don't, and he has to prepare his next play and lose some of his profits the while. Into a category of ' moderate success ' ninety per cent of profitable productions will fall. And here, while the long-run manager has still no great cause of complaint, the repertory system begins, in comparison, to show its advantages. A theatre with a capacity of £300 a performance, of £2,400 a week (of eight performances), may take only £1,400 and still make a pleasant profit. But, obviously, if the £1,400 worth of audience can be—as it could be—accommodated in five performances, this would be better business. And this is what repertory sets out to do, and can do. There will, we may admit, always be a small margin of loss—of the playgoer who can go at one time but not at another, or who suddenly finds himself with an evening free and if the play is not ' on tap ' then will take no more trouble about it. But this, for the sort of plays a National Theatre would be concerned with, *is* a small margin.

The principle of the repertory system lies in the adjusting of the number of performances given to the number of people who wish to see the play. And, as we descend in the scale of ' long-run ' success, through moderate to small profits, to barely paying business, to business which just covers current outgoings and leaves the production cost a dead loss, to losing business in which there still seems some hope, or in which there is none, though the loss is less than the loss on an empty theatre would be—all these gradations having to be calculated in terms of a theatre open for eight performances, staffed for eight performances, advertised for eight performances, with its waste of empty seats, and the rest of the waste—at every step of the descent the long-run system shows up worse and the repertory better. There may be three thousand people a week wanting to see a play, and the loss on long-run terms will still be catastrophic; while if one thousand people want to see it in a repertory, one performance can be given at a good profit.

The financial problem in the theatre lies mainly

in the eliminating of this margin of waste, and the repertory system shows us the way. With the long-run there is little between the high plateau of handsome profit and the plunge into preposterous loss. The repertory provides a gradual slope upon which plays of every degree of attractiveness can find a paying place.

With concerts and opera the public is already used to the essentials of the system; no one dreams of complaining that *The Meistersingers* is not produced for a run, or that you cannot hear Beethoven six nights a week at the Promenades. The theatre public, the more thoughtless part of it, would need a little accustoming to the change; but, if the thing were done boldly and the fare offered the best, this should not take long.

The system will not work with automatic perfection, of course; there must always be errors of judgment. But, announcing the repertory for but a fortnight ahead (and few people want to foresee such engagements for further), these should never be very serious. The management will learn how to feel the pulse of its public. At the worst a new production will be billed for six performances when it should only have had two or three. On the other hand there is no reason that a settled success should not be announced for three or four definite performances a week for a couple of months to come.

Lastly, in looking at these estimates it should be remembered that they are of *average* receipts. There would, on occasions, no doubt, be houses half full or even less. If no experiments were made the management would be much to blame; if none of them failed, it would be superhuman. But the theatre would be in a bad way indeed if none of the forty-nine plays drew full houses in compensation.

While I am correcting proofs two pertinent pieces of information reach me. The first is from Mr. H. M. Harwood, who tells me that his own receipts over a period of about ten years—balancing successes against failures upon the long-run system —" are about ten per cent less than two-thirds."* The second is from Lord Lytton about the ' Old Vic,' of whose governing body he is Chairman, and I quote it verbatim. " The first few nights of every new Shakespeare performance are rather poorly attended. On the last three nights we always have to turn a large number away. We have a clientele which comes regularly to all the plays, but the wider public waits for a report that the new play is a success, and many who put off applying for seats till the last moment find that they cannot get in. Allowing for this habit of the public, our average Shakespeare attendance throughout the year is about 900 out of a seating capacity of 1,600. For opera, on the other hand, the theatre is always full, and we turn people away every night."

The pertinence of this is obvious. Shakespeare, at the ' Old Vic,' is put on for interrupted runs of two or three weeks to each play. This incurs the disadvantages without the advantages of the long-run system; but even so the average attendance is not so far under two-thirds capacity. Opera, on the other hand, is inserted in the bill upon a method akin to the repertory system—and the theatre is always full!

* For some qualification of this, and for more of his observations, see Appendix I, p. 121.

CHAPTER XIII

ADDITIONAL TAKINGS

Refreshment-room profits   £5,000

T H E R E are other very possible sources of extra revenue, ranging from special performances given in other cities, and work that might be done for the B.B.C. (if and when small units of the company could be detached without prejudice to the main programme), to the small profits of a bookstall. But as these would mostly involve extra outlay it is better not to bring them into present calculations.

The refreshment-rooms, however, would be a certain source of income. We are estimating for the entertaining of more than 800,000 people a year. If the National Theatre were not to be a ' no fee ' theatre (but it should be), some refreshment contractor could easily be found who would be willing enough to pay £5,000 a year and more for the privilege of selling them programmes at 6d. and 3d. apiece, and many cups of tea and whiskies-and-soda. He would at the same time relieve the theatre of the £6,240, the estimated cost of cloak-room attendants and ushers. But he will not pay £5,000 for the chance of doing something which will cost him nearly another £7,000 a year to do (refreshment-room salaries are not included in the £6,240) unless he sees profit in it, and more than would come from the programmes and their advertisements. Quite apart from this one item—which the theatre would renounce—the refreshment-rooms could be made to pay well; more particularly such refreshment-rooms as are in the building plan that we have been considering. Most theatres can provide nothing but an easily crowded bar and tea-trays to be precariously balanced on the knee. But with spacious rooms and good service (the plan even provides a grill-room which could operate before and after performances) there is no reason whatever that the theatre itself should not give its programmes and cloak-room service for nothing, extract the saved sixpences and much more from its clients for eatables and drinkables, and find itself with a tidy sum to the good. We have allowed for the cost of the programmes and of all but the actual refreshment-room staff. This £5,000 can safely be set on the credit side.

CHAPTER XIV

SUMMARY OF EXPENSES AND TAKINGS
PREPARATION EXPENSES

Expenses

	£
Directorate (chap. iv)	9,750
Salaries in front of house (chap. ix)	18,966
Salaries at back of house (chap. ix)	20,831
Salaries of company (chap. vi)	75,200
Yearly allotment of production costs (chap. vii)	33,250
Music (chap. x)	9,400
General expenses (chap. xi)	21,800
Authors' fees and pension fund (chap. viii)	20,460
	£209,657

Takings

	£
Large House ⎱ (chap. xii)	128,920
Small House ⎰	75,680
Profit on refreshments (chap. xiii)	5,000
	£209,600

By which it would appear that the theatre will be making a loss on its bare working of £57 a year!

But, of course, these estimates cannot, and do not, pretend to such accuracy. They should suffice to show, however—and this is all their claim—that the enterprise is, upon this scale and with the arbitrary allowances made, financially feasible. Various economies could be contrived, but the whole effect of them could hardly be very great. Some increase of cost might well find its compensation in higher receipts if—but only if—the plays and performances were the best of their kind. Everything finally depends on this; on the faith that there will always be an educated audience for good drama once it is provided.

Preliminary endowment is necessary, and upon a generous scale; that must not be shirked. The upkeep of the building and of the permanent equipment had better be provided for, though it might not be needed. No further subsidy should be required. If it were, then, at the worst—if these estimates have any claim to validity—it could be confined within definite and probably quite narrow limits. At the best this loss of £57 a year might even be turned into an equivalent profit. And a bigger one should not be aimed at.

Preparation

These estimates (once again) are for a normal year, with the theatre in full working order, and two or three years at least would be needed for this whipping into shape. It is not to be supposed, for instance, that anything like fifty productions could be staged in the first year, nor anything like 880 performances given. But it would be better to begin working with the two houses from the beginning, even if they could not be simultaneously open; for here, as we have seen, is an essential part of the theatre's artistic and economic machinery, and its use must be learnt, both by the staff and the actors, and the public.

But there would need to be preparation before

the theatre was opened at all. First, a company must be integrated, though not the full company. One sees the selecting of between thirty and forty young, not too inexperienced, actors and actresses, the adding of half a dozen of more weight, and the setting of the lot (with further additions now and then to compensate for inevitable subtractions) to a couple of years' hard gruelling at Shakespeare, eighteenth-century comedy and a number of modern plays. Let there be as much study and rehearsal in proportion to performance as possible. The two main objects should be, to accustom the actors to each other and to develop a common method. If it would not be too discouraging a whole year might well be devoted to the study of Shakespeare's verse and how to speak it—how to compass the half-dozen different developments of it—before ever a performance was given. Here would be a need for subsidy; but the expenditure of money and time would be profitable; it would indeed be necessary. One could no more open the National Theatre with an untrained and unaccustomed company than go into battle with a well-intentioned, undisciplined mob, a regiment in name only.

But to admit and plead for this (and it should ask no argument) is by no means to advocate the setting up of a company on trial, with all question of its establishment in a suitable theatre left dependent upon some arbitrary estimate of its success. The difference between the two projects is vital, and not the less because it would largely consist of imponderable things. To gather a company and set them to such drastic work with a definite end plainly in view, with their theatre already building for their reception, is one matter. To try to rally them with " If . . . If . . . If! " would be very much another. There could be no recruiting of actors and producers and staff of the right quality, nor any heart in the work, unless they knew that it was not to be a ploughing of the sands.

CHAPTER XV

TRIBUTARY ENTERPRISES

The Question of a Training School

W H E N, some twenty-seven years ago, the *Scheme and Estimates* were drawn up, there existed in England no dramatic school of any consequence, and we planned the establishing of one in close connection with the theatre. For, clearly, well-trained recruits will be needed. But there are now flourishing not one, but several schools of reputation. The Royal Academy of Dramatic Art, in particular, is a public institution with a Royal Charter, and The Central School of Speech Training (an incorporated body) covers even wider ground. To set up yet another school would be foolish. There are, moreover, definite advantages both in keeping would-be recruits to the theatre from falling too much under its influence during the time of their training, and in that training being as varied as thoroughness allows.

As things are now, then, a National Theatre's best policy would seem to be to enter into relations with certain schools of recognised competence, those, for instance, that the University of London already recognises in its scheme for granting diplomas in dramatic art. From them it could require the services of a certain number of ' third year ' students for ' walking-on ' and (possibly) understudying; and it will be remembered that £2,000 a year has been set aside for the payment of their expenses. In return there might be offered yearly from three to six one-year engagements, to be competed for by the students of these schools. The theatre could not undertake to recruit from no other sources; but it stands to reason that perfectly untrained actors would be of no use to it.

It might be well for the theatre to be represented upon the governing bodies of these schools, so that it could have a say in the matter of the curriculum.

Relations with the British Broadcasting Corporation

Possibly some useful work might be done for the B.B.C. The technique of the broadcast play is still a matter of experiment; but whatever else may or may not be needed for it, good speech certainly will be; and in this a National Theatre must specialise, or be unworthy of its name. It should indeed become a court of appeal in this matter. Whether it could advantageously help in the actual experimenting is for the B.B.C. to say. But it certainly could, without much disturbance to its main work, detach from time to time members of the company, whose value for the broadcasting of certain plays would be very great.

An Empire Touring Company

The National Theatre Company could not, as a whole, ever go on tour.* This is sufficiently obvious when one looks at the salary list and considers the cost of transport, considers too the rapid depreciation of the scenery and furniture which would have to be carried round; no possible provincial receipts would compensate. Nor could the company very well be sent travelling for long in sections. What-

* I do not say that a three months' season in that Eldorado, New York, might not be arranged; but even here there would be no commensurate profit.

113   I

ever profits they made would be seriously eaten into—if not altogether eaten up—by the maintenance cost of the empty theatre they would leave behind (or if that were let, by the cost of such permanent staff as could not be employed), and by the cost of the rehearsals that would be needed when they were re-united before they could begin to act as a whole again.

But there is no reason whatever why a touring company (more than one, even) should not be attached to the theatre, and much is to be said in favour of the plan. From the theatre's point of view, it would be another means to the granting of those important ' furloughs ' by which actors are to be saved from staleness and from financial and artistic discontent. Those who wanted to spend their year raking in extra large sums of money could not be expected to join it; but there would be those to whom the theatre could not quickly enough give the leading parts which they might think—and justifiably—they deserved, who would be glad to go playing them round England, or, better, in Canada, South Africa, India, Australia or some of the Colonies for a year, whom the theatre would be glad to see so playing them, for they would come back with their value to it increased. And the touring company could recruit besides from the young actors engaged by the year, who could not always hope for immediate promotion to permanent engagements.

Such a company had better be financially, and, in the main, administratively, independent. The theatre machine, as we have planned it, is already amply large for easy working. But the connection could be close. The National Theatre could provide offices, the hospitality, probably, of rehearsal rooms, the occasional services of producers, contingent rights in plays, the help, very often, of its costume and scene stores.

From the larger, the cultural and political point of view, one need not insist upon the value of such a company, carrying (with some of the prestige that one hopes the National Theatre would soon earn) its representative repertory of good English plays throughout the Empire. It would surely not lack a welcome; nor financial guarantees, one may suppose. And, in these days of increasing political independence, it would stand as the symbol of a cultural unity, a beneficent bond.

APPENDIX I

CRITICISMS AND ANSWERS

I H A V E had, of course, expert help in drawing up these estimates, my chief adviser being Mr. Walter Peacock, to whom here again I tender my thanks—I should have been sadly at a loss without him. Nevertheless, he is not to be held responsible for them as they stand, in gross or detail. If the premises are his the conclusions are often wholly mine, and on the basis of his actual and accurate figures I have built an imaginary structure which he has every right to disown. He is, however, I think, in general sympathy with the scheme—with some such scheme as this, at any rate.

So are many other prominent workers for the theatre, actors, dramatists, managers; the names of some of them will be found in the list which forms a postscript to the Preface. But the job being roughly done, I turned for criticism not to them, but to others whom I knew to be more or less out of sympathy with the very idea of a National Theatre—and I asked them to show no mercy. Even greater gratitude then, in a sense, is due to them for spending their time in commenting upon what they can only consider to have been a waste of mine. But they speak with much authority, and what they say can hardly be complaisant.

Upon certain points, I found, their criticisms cancelled each other out. This was pleasing. But it does not follow in such cases that anyone concerned is in the wrong, only that—

> There are nine and sixty ways of constructing
>   tribal lays
> And every single one of them is right.

117

Upon other points their objections were rather to the thing in itself than to my estimate of its cost; and again —where no estimates are possible, as in the case of the theatre's likely receipts—to my assumptions. I put on record what they say, and such evidence as I can muster to contradict it.

Upon many other—but mostly minor—points the criticism was so pertinent that it simply had to be met by a readjustment of figures. I was determined—making whatever allowances were necessary—to show something like a balanced budget. In admitting that a number of items were underestimated, I had to distribute a sum of £6,000 which was to have served—but might still have been insufficient—for rates and taxes and upkeep of equipment. In recording these criticisms I have shown by an asterisk (*) when I have thus done something to meet them. It does not follow that by this something they have been nullified; but I fancy that in most cases the sting is now out of them.

Without quoting verbatim I have tried to present the objections fairly; and more casual critics of the scheme will find, I'm sure, that this very expert criticism saves them a lot of trouble. While for those who advocate a National Theatre nothing is more important than to know what informed criticism they have to meet—a very different thing from factious opposition—and to discover how they can meet it. My answers to the objections made I print in italics.

Sir Alfred Butt, upon the assumption that the premise is right, that a National Theatre is desirable (as to which he does not commit himself personally one way or the other), thinks that the case is well set out. His one concrete criticism of the figures—he does not deal with them in detail—is that £4,500 is insufficient pay for the Director. He thinks that the position would have to carry at least £7,000 a year.

Mr. Horace Watson was, perhaps, my harshest critic; but so convincing upon many points—and his experience, within its range, is unrivalled—that, as will be seen by the asterisks, he drove me to one minor amendment after another.

He does not, to begin with, believe that there is any general demand for a National Theatre, or that it would do very much for the drama. He says also that if it were established, so much would depend upon the site, the nature of the building and the conditions of tenancy, that accurate estimates of the cost of its working cannot be made. *This is indisputable; but the objection applies mainly to the cost of the staff, less to the costs of production, somewhat to the question of advertisement and the chances of receipts, but hardly at all to the large items of actors' salaries.*

He thinks the Director would be hard to get (agrees that within his sphere he should be an autocrat and does not envy him the job) and, with Sir Alfred Butt, harder to get for the money. *I did first put him down at £5,000 instead of £4,500.*

He says " possibly yes " to the salaries of the Business and Literary managers.

He thinks the salaries of Acting Managers*, Stage Managers* and heads of departments generally* are considerably underestimated. *I have in some instances increased them appreciably; but I think the criticism did not always take pension prospects into account.*

He insists that the box-office staff must be very much increased*—*I have given fairly full effect to this*—and that there would be far more secretarial work to do*. He thinks that money-takers*, check-takers* and cleaners* must be added to, and that probably more stage hands would be needed. *As to this last I made no change, for I have calculated upon machinery ousting labour as far as possible.*

As to the actors and their salaries, he emphasises the

difficulties which I have emphasised; but, these apart, does not quarrel much with the estimates.

He expresses no definite opinion upon the costs of production, but, from figures he has been good enough to show me, we cannot be in serious disagreement.

He thinks the orchestra could hardly be recruited for that sum, with that amount of work to do, says the conductor would be underpaid*—*without raising the salary I have added fees for composing incidental music*—also the leader*. *I raised the salary by £200, and may have fully met this criticism.*

He thinks the general expenses tend to be underestimated; in particular advertisement*—*This item I have since increased by £1,000 a year. One can spend anything on advertisement; I do not propose that the National Theatre should do more than give the public adequate information*—lighting and heating*—*I added another £1,000 here. The cost of this must largely depend on the nature of the building; but I think the sum now allowed is probably sufficient*—and printing.

When it comes to probable receipts he thinks the estimate of an average taking of two-thirds the theatre's capacity ' unduly optimistic,' and, as will be seen, other critics agree with him. *Here I must—for reasons set out at length in the body of the book—definitely join issue. They argue, I think, too much from ' long-run ' premises, invalid with repertory. The statistics of foreign repertory theatres—for all the post-war disorganisation, social and financial—still tend to prove the case. And if it is hard to compare one country with another, there is in England the parallel with the Opera, and the evidence of the mixed opera and short-run Shakespeare at the Old Vic, set out in Lord Lytton's letter on p. 105. It might take the larger London public a little time to accustom itself to the system. But there is no reason in nature that it should not. And without this—it is as well to face it—there can be no running of such a theatre upon any reasonable economic basis.*

APPENDIX I

But it is interesting to note how experience, in general and particular, differs even within the limits of the long-run system. Mr. Watson thinks that an average taking of two-thirds capacity is not to be expected, but Mr. H. M. Harwood (p. 105), working in a small theatre it is true, records his receipts over ten years at " about ten per cent less than two-thirds." I state (p. 99), as justification for pricing half the seats, or more, in a National Theatre at 5s. and 2s. 6d., that " when any play of quality is produced in London, seats at about these prices are the first to fill and the last to empty." Mr. Watson and Mr. Alec Rea, who have produced many plays of quality, do not agree. Mr. Watson says: " There is no one part of the theatre which fills quicker than another or empties sooner. Assuming success, it may be taken generally that the whole theatre at all prices sells quickly. After that . . . the higher-priced seats begin to go first and the lower ones last, but they all go proportionately together. Occasionally one may find that the lower-priced seats are slower in leaving than the higher ones, and that one can substitute the lower-priced seats for the higher ones and still keep the theatre filled, but in practice that does not last for very long." Mr. Alec Rea says categorically: " My experience is that our Upper Circle is always the last place to fill and the first to empty, and at the St. Martin's they are fairly good seats." Mr. Harwood's experience, in a theatre next door, traverses this. Mr. Cochran, with his recent remarkable production of The Silver Tassie, *found that his 5s. and 2s. 6d. customers crowded in for long after the 10s. 6d. ones began to prove faithless. And Sir Barry Jackson quotes to me productions of* Hamlet (*in modern dress*), *Henri Ghéon's* St. Bernard, Six Characters in Search of an Author, *and* Back to Methuselah ('*highbrow' plays all, certainly—except* Hamlet!) *as filling and overfilling cheaper seats, while the dearer ones were emptying.*

Mr. Alec Rea and Mr. Clift (Mr. Rea premising that he

is " opposed to the whole scheme ") think that the £200,000 demanded as a contingent fund for accumulating the material of productions and supporting the theatre during a three years' apprenticeship to its task would all be definitely sunk. *Yes, it might be.*

They approve the salaries to be paid to the Director and the General Staff.

They approve also of those set down for the actors with the caveat that it might be hard to obtain ' leading ' actors—*they do not comment upon the ' furlough ' plan, on which I should greatly rely*—and those in whom the public is interested—*as to which I must answer that it would be for the theatre itself to be interesting, the whole greater than its parts.*

They question the theatre's chances of obtaining new and popular plays.

They dispute the lowering of the costs of production by twenty to twenty-five per cent, compared to contract prices, by doing the work in the theatre's own (rent-free) workshops. *But it seems to me indisputable that this much could be saved, provided that the staff could be kept steadily at work. And upon this question Mr. Harwood goes further than I do.*

They think, in consequence, and in view of a certain number of ' big ' productions, that it would be safer to raise the average cost of a production in the larger house by £1,000. *But I fancy they must have in mind more expensively ' carpentered ' productions of Shakespeare and other costume plays than I myself see the National Theatre indulging in. I believe, indeed, that, except where an appearance of opulence and even extravagance in a production is itself an attraction, and where the play alone would never be, the day for this sort of thing has definitely gone by. We have come through it and out on the other side. All has been done that can be done, and the Cinema can do so much more. The Russian Ballet, which had to travel and could not carry vast quantities of carpentry about, taught us again how much can be done by good design and clever painting—a far more thrifty method.*

They approve in general the salaries of the staff and even suggest some economies—*on my original figures, that is to say, not those which now appear in the book. They should find a few of these on the extravagant side. But, it is safer, I feel, to put such estimates up and hope for a few pleasant surprises, than to reduce them and risk unpleasant ones.*

They thought the estimate for advertisements was hardly high enough*.

They suggest that even if programmes are given away some revenue could be had from advertisements in them. *I should regret the disfigurement.* As to receipts I have quoted part of their opinion above. For the rest they fasten upon the 150 or more Shakespearean performances a year and think that an average receipt of one-third capacity for these is all that could be looked for. *The experience of the Old Vic—with cheaper prices truly, but with productions of a lower standard than a National Theatre could give—is against them in this.*

They call attention, however, to what is, I agree, a real danger—that the ' obligatory ' performances of Shakespeare might become a weariness to the public's flesh and be very sparsely attended. *There is indeed a danger here: though one must not exaggerate it. The ' classic ' performances at the Comédie Française are, I think, always very full. It would be for the Director to see that these performances were not perfunctory, but interesting in themselves. Further I should hope—see p.* 101—*that for these in particular there would be organised audiences of students and school children.*

They query the appeal that revivals of plays twenty to ten years old can make to the public. *I agree that revivals for a run seldom justify themselves; but when ten performances in a repertory are all you need to give, it may be a very different matter.*

Mr. H. M. Harwood first questions whether such an enterprise must not grow from a small beginning. *I have in the body of the book given my reasons for disagreeing with him—though, of course, I do not totally disagree with him. But no one, I suppose, sees the enterprise starting at full blast.*

He thinks that though a theatre built for the purpose is an ultimate ideal, it cannot reasonably be asked for while there is a chance of utter failure. *I can only answer that the theatre would, I think, have no chance of success unless it were provided with the establishment and equipment it needs; no chance of economic success at any rate, nor very much of a comprehensive artistic success. But granted artistic success: this is almost always won in such cases by some strenuous effort which it is humanly impossible to sustain. And it would only be greeted with: Excellent! Go on as you are.*

He approves the plan for the government of the theatre. He thinks the salaries of the General Staff reasonable, and wholly approves of the triumvirate for the selection of plays, speaking—and it is worth quotation—of the need to " keep the thing a living organisation as distinct from a museum. You cannot build, or keep alive, a theatrical organisation on dead men's bones, of whatever quality. Your major concern must be the tilling of new ground, even if the soil is a little less rich."

Referring to the tentative plan of the building he considers the stages are unnecessarily large. *I agree; but Mr. Somerville was given a very spacious site to work to for the purposes of the competition.*

He thinks that there should be not two houses only, but three, the extra one being very small and inexpensive to run, fitted to really experimental work.* *I think it an excellent idea if space could be found.*

He thinks that the company is needlessly large and that some of the larger casts could be filled by outsider

* See p. 52.

specially engaged. *I feel sure that this is both impracticable and undesirable.*

He thinks that some of the intermediate salaries are unnecessarily high. *They just possibly may be; but on the whole I disagree, for reasons given in the body of the book.*

With regard to production costs he thinks—as against Mr. Rea and Mr. Clift—that the theatre having its own workshops, my estimates of these might be considerably reduced.

He is for a uniform rate of author's royalties, but thinks that five per cent up to £1,000 worth of receipts and ten per cent on any excess—the calculation to be made presumably per eight performances—would suffice, his argument being that London rights only are nowadays of comparatively small importance, the author reaping his chief harvest from American, Continental and Film rights. If these are left to him he would be actually better off than with higher terms from a manager who asked for a share in them. *My objections are two. Managers ask for these contingent interests more often than they get them. A fair proportion of the plays produced might not be marketable for the films, or even in America.*

Cost of advertising. He does not dispute the estimate for this as things are. But he insists that, once a National Theatre were established, the newspapers would announce its daily programme for nothing—as they now do for the B.B.C. and for racing and football matches. He insists, indeed, that, as it is information, every theatre has a claim to such a bare announcement free. *It is true, I think, that in the old days of ' Under the Clock ' they always had it.*

Besides these detailed criticisms, Mr. Harwood set out for me his opinion upon the matter as a whole in a letter from which I quote verbatim; each point that he so shrewdly makes asks, I think, for an answer. I do my best.

" I am not, naturally, an active opponent. Indeed, why should I, or anyone, be that? But I am in complete agreement with both Rea and Watson in my doubt as to a National Theatre serving any useful purpose so far as the progress and encouragement of the drama is concerned."

. . . Without admitting this, there would still remain the task of keeping alive the good drama, old and modern, which already exists, the providing of the equivalent of a library of standard literature. Private enterprise makes no attempt to do so, and the situation inevitably becomes worse every year.

" The percentage of new works of any importance that have been given their first hearing at any State-aided theatre in the last twenty-five years must be very small. And indeed the very nature of the institution is likely to preclude this. Nor, if you look back over the period of your own experience, does it seem likely that such a theatre in England would have bettered the record in this respect. Would a National Theatre have produced Ibsen in the early 'nineties? Or Shaw in 1905? Or even *The Second Mrs. Tanqueray?* Or *Justice, Waste, The Silver Box* and *The Voysey Inheritance—when they were written?* I don't believe it for a moment. The countries with State theatres have not been the ones to do the most interesting work in the last twenty-five years, and when they have done something noticeable, it has not been done in the State Theatre. So much for experience." *There is some force in this, of course. But it is partly conjecture; and, for the rest, experience does not wholly support the contention. State theatres in Scandinavia and Germany did do Ibsen in the early 'nineties, and long before. In France the Comédie (until it produced a one-act play by Barrie the other day) has made a rule of never doing any modern foreign drama at all. But German State theatres were doing Shaw while he was still in the hands of the Stage Society over here. I do not deny that the tendency of academies is to be academic, but one jumps to conclusions in this direction at one's peril. Writing an article the other day upon the Comédie Française, I referred to an excellent revival of* Les Corbeaux, *and said what a pity it was that*

Becque and the French drama generally had lacked the encouragement of its production there when it was written. A correspondent promptly pointed out that the play was originally produced at the Comédie. Mr. Harwood surely slips when he says that the countries with State theatres have not been the ones to do the most interesting work in the last twenty-five years, for there are State theatres in every European country except England, Italy and Spain—where by no means the most interesting work has been done. (The case of America must be argued separately. There all traditions and conditions are against public enterprise and in favour of private.) When he adds that in these countries the most interesting work has been done elsewhere than in the State theatres themselves, may it not just possibly be—paradoxical as this may seem—that one of the uses of an academy is to provide the independents and the younger school with something solid to measure their strength against: just as undoubtedly one of the incidental benefits His Majesty's Government must confer on the country lies in giving occasion and opportunity for His Majesty's Opposition to criticise it. Nothing does more to stimulate good government than an effective opposition: but an opposition's first need is to have something to oppose. I fully admit that we owe much—though not quite all—of the pioneer work done during the last generation in Russia, Germany and France, and much that directly followed from it, to Stanislawsky and Meyerhold, Brahm and Reinhardt, Antoine, Lugné-Poe and Copeau. But how far were not their hands strengthened by the fact that their public had first been nourished upon a tradition of sound ' academic ' work? All this without for a moment admitting that a National Theatre need be retrograde or even blindly conservative. Instances enough can be found to the contrary: the Royal Theatre at Copenhagen for one, the famous Saxe-Meiningen company for another.

" *Theoretically*, I happen to be one of the last remaining mug-wumps who believe that State interference in any

form of human activity, beyond what is absolutely necessary, is disastrous. I have served on a public (municipal)
body, and can conceive no form of enterprise less suited to
public control than theatrical production. You yourself
are aware of this, and deprecate—very wisely—bureaucratic interference. But what chance have you of such
freedom? If this theatre is to be a success it must be something in which your citizens take a lively interest, otherwise it cannot live. Is it to be believed that they will con-
sent to a dictatorship that may not be to their liking? Once,
or twice, if you happen to get the right man, possibly, but
not for long. You cannot keep your shareholders (for that
is what they are) permanently gagged if you're doing something they don't like.

"The argument from the National Gallery and Museums
is fallacious. *They* are not challenging public opinion every
two or three weeks, and are confessedly concerned with
preserving rather than making a standard. Nor are the
numbers of citizens who are interested in them in *any* way
comparable to the numbers who would have to be interested
in your theatre if it is to be a going concern. I do not believe for a moment that you could hope to keep yourself
free from the meddling of bureaucracy and—in the last
resort—of politicians."

*With the intention of all this I agree most heartily. Political
interferences and external bureaucratic control would be fatal.
But I believe that Mr. Harwood both misreads the signs of the
times and takes too partial a view of the disposition of the
public. Throughout most of the last century our individualists
had their way, and now our socialists have had their say:
and, as a result, if one thing is politically certain it is that
neither pure individualism nor pure socialism is going, in the
future, to provide a method for the government of England.
The problem of to-day is to discover how, in public enterprises,
the necessary virtues of both can be combined. English-fashion,
we are giving the doctrinaires the go-by and seeking a solution*

128

*for each separate case. We find one more often than appears;
for the moment a plan works no more is heard of it. A pity,
perhaps, that any act must be organised; but the theatre, of
all others, cannot escape this fate. It really need not pass the
wit of man to devise a constitution for the National Theatre
which will give it, in sufficiently equal measure, both security
and freedom. As to the public taking too lively an interest in
its doings—why, that is a danger to be courted. The accustomed objection is, of course, that no one would care a dump
what the theatre did, and whether it lived or died. The
complaint in Paris is that the public is altogether too acquiescent towards the faults and failings of the National
Theatres, that they crowd to them whatever is done. No, the
livelier the criticism of its work, the healthier the condition of
the enterprise would be—and the more prosperous. For Mr.
Harwood forgets, I think, what a great variety of work such
a theatre would be compelled to do. Granted that it was all
good of its kind (when it wasn't, well, no one would wish to
save it), there are all kinds of audiences to be pleased, varying
in numbers as in taste. Is not violent abuse by one set of critics
the surest sign that another set, and the public they represent,
will soon be as loud in praise? An easy tolerance is the thing
to be dreaded. The director could take for his motto the old
tag* Divide et impera.

" I feel that the whole issue is clouded by the name of
Shakespeare. The first thing everyone postulates is a
'place where you can see Shakespeare's plays.' Most of the
advocates' ideas on what the theatre is to do seem to go
little beyond this. That does not interest me much. Is it
maintained that work that ought to be done by new men
is failing to get produced, and that such work *would* be done
by a National Theatre? It is true only to a very limited degree
that good original work cannot get a hearing, and I gravely
doubt whether your national committee would take a very
different view of these rejected play from that taken by the
various individual managers under the present system."

This is sound criticism, I think. We do want a place where we can see Shakespeare's plays, and we shall not know how much we want it till we see them there well done. But we do him and his work and the whole cause the worst possible service by making a fetish of him. People bow down, and say in their hearts: What a bore! The National Theatre's business will be to give us the best drama of every sort, and Shakespeare's only because it is among the best. Will good original drama find more chance of a hearing there than it has now? Possibly not. When it does get heard there it should certainly be more effectively heard. But, doubtless, year in and year out, this cry will need to be raised; and nothing will be better for the theatre itself than to have the younger generation insistently knocking at its door.

" All this won't help you, of course, except in so far as you'll have to answer something of the sort to someone, and I certainly think you're wise in collecting all the ' contras ' so that you can destroy them at your leisure! " *There is no greater help than such criticism towards clearing the mind of cant.*

" As for the politicians, if any of these gentlemen, of whatever persuasion, tries to ' acquire merit ' by posing as the friend of the drama, he will hear something in due course from the practitioners of an industry which he and his kind have done their best to ruin by their fantastic taxation."

I hold no brief here for any politician, except the one who will do his part in establishing the National Theatre. And for that his sins—even his share in the levying of the entertainment tax—shall, as far as I am concerned, be forgiven him.

APPENDIX II

STATE-AIDED THEATRES ABROAD

O N E must be wary in drawing conclusions from even the fullest statistics of the working of foreign theatres, so much in which they differ from English ones goes unrecorded. Since the war, moreover, state-aided theatres in the combatant countries have inevitably shared the financial difficulties of their Governments. They have many of them—and as inevitably—fallen into administrative confusion besides. With constitutions already out of date, and one obligation after another piled up on them as payment for State support, they were often hard put to it even by 1914 to adjust the fictions of their existence to economic realities; and since then, it is needless to say, these troubles have multiplied. It says everything, both for the devotion of the men and women who work in them and for the public's regard for them, that they have not during these last twelve difficult years closed their doors altogether. But they stand traditionally as an integral part of the social life of their cities; and governments, facing bankruptcy, have still felt compelled to do something to help them out. The something has usually been so many extra francs or marks or kröne, and the one thing needful, a thorough reorganisation of their working rules, has mostly been left undone. If we look abroad, therefore, for lessons in the organising of our own National Theatre, we shall at the moment find examples enough of what not to do. But do not let us argue from this that state-aided theatres are a failure. The conclusion should rather be that, were they not, in the best sense of the word, a success, did they not supply a generally admitted need, they could not be surviving—as they

131

are, and, all said and done, with surprising credit—their present intolerable hardships.

The notes and statistics which follow make no pretence to fullness, though they are not, I think, inaccurate. They give such fragmentary information as I have been able casually to gather during the rather hurried writing of this book; information with enough bearing upon its problems to be of some use, I think, to those who wish to reconsider them.

The Comédie Française, eldest and best reputed of all State theatres, is struggling at the moment with a variety of difficulties. It is still ostensibly governed under the famous Decree of Moscow, an instrument which surely owes more to Napoleon's reputation than to its own wisdom, which is, in any case, as out of date to-day as the guns behind which it was written. It entangles Administrateur and Sociétaires in a complex of responsibilities, sets one interest jarring with another, and must need, for its tolerable working, a rich margin, so to speak, of prosperity, upon which everyone concerned may be fed to satisfaction —almost any system will work then. To copy such a constitution would be sheer lunacy. The lesson to be learned is that the fewer and the less rigid the rules under which such a theatre is governed the better; and, one may add, if a tithe of the tales be true, the further it is removed from political interference the healthier it will be.

The Comédie, then, is crying aloud for financial and administrative reorganisation, and, meanwhile, is in no condition to face the inevitable troubles of the time.

It has an overgrown and underpaid company; overgrown and underpaid because it is for the most part underworked; underworked because it has but the one stage and one house to occupy. Individual actors are always taking *congés* here, there and everywhere; the government expects whole sections of the company to be sent from time to time on propagandist tours; the disorganisation is terrible.

The stage is poorly equipped; there are no proper rehearsal rooms; the current repertory (so-called) must look after itself.

The theatre is not over large; but while there seldom seem to be any seats free, except the very bad ones, of which ʳthere are too many, the cheap prices and the *abonnement* reduce the receipts. The present subvention of 1,000,000 francs (£8,064)—till recently it was but half this—is illusory. The State and the city of Paris between them must take back more in taxes.* The *Comédie Française*, indeed, except for its own accumulated funds, is not, at the moment, a subventioned theatre at all.

But, for all this, the theatre fills night after night. And though one may see regrettably bad performances there, and far too many of them, there are others as excellent to redress the balance. At the moment of writing, a most instructive programme may be seen, consisting of Alfred de Musset's *Les Caprices de Marianne* and Rostand's *Les Romanesques*. The first is intolerably badly done and bores the audience to extinction, an audience that is crowding to see the second, a production which, without being perfect, is every bit as good as it needs to be, and far better upon several counts than any other theatre in Paris could make it. Here, then, in an evening, we may see on the one hand a National Theatre as it quite obviously need never become; or, on the other, we have it—with no great trouble or expense, no rallying of its most famous actors—showing all its quality.

Prussia seems to subsidise its State theatres far more heavily. Comparisons are difficult and (once again) not

* In a most informative article in the *Observer*, Mr. Philip Carr recently pointed out that the subvention stood at 240,000 francs in 1840 when the franc was worth about ten times as much as it is to-day. The subvention, that is to say, is really two-fifths of what it was then; and taxes, as well as real prices, are higher.

very significant. One may set against the French 7,639,459 francs (£61,609) a year (1929), which includes support for the Opera and its library, the Conservatoire of music and a fair amount of assistance for popular concerts and the like, the Prussian budget (1928) for Berlin of 6,919,561 marks (£338,696), which supports two Operas and is supposed to support two theatres.* In both cases, of course, Opera takes a far larger share of the money. The administration of the Prussian State theatres is, however, now being drastically reorganised.

Austria devotes (1929) 5,270,950 Austrian schillings (£152,406) to the Opera and two theatres in Vienna, the *Burgtheater* and the *Akademietheater*.

The average receipts per performance for the season 1928/29 (prices not ruling, I think, very high) were—

The Opera	12,094 Austrian schillings			(£349)
Burgtheater	5,423	,,	,,	(£157)
Akademietheater	2,763	,,	,,	(£80)

Dr. Hevesi, Director of the National Theatre in Budapest, gives me some very interesting information.

He has a company numbering 67, and the pupils of the Theatrical Academy can be called upon besides for the playing of minor parts.

He has two houses, and considers this a necessity if the energies of the company are to be fully absorbed.

He stages from 85 to 90 different plays a year, 20 to 25 of them being new productions (either new plays or freshly staged revivals).

He has a subsidy of 800,000 pengö (about £30,000) a year.

The larger house, when full, holds about £150. The prices are not high. They are proportionately higher in the

* The Schauspielhaus and the Schiller Theatre; but the latter has been rented since 1923.

small house, which (as far as the interests of the two can be separated) seems to absorb little or none of the subsidy.

The receipts from November to March average 80 to 85 per cent of the theatre's capacity. Other months do not show up so well, and May and June are practically a dead season. Even so the general average does not fall lower than between 60 and 70 per cent.

The theatre has (I may add) a very great reputation both within Hungary and without.

The Westminster Press
411a Harrow Road
London W.9